D0865405

On Holiday in the Lake District

On Holiday in the Lake District

WORDSWORTH'S
GATEWAY

Dalesman Books
1981

The Dalesman Publishing Company Ltd.,
Clapham, via Lancaster, LA2 8EB

First published 1981

© Dalesman Publishing Company Ltd., 1981

ISBN: 0 85206 640 6

Printed by Galava Printing Company Limited, Nelson, Lancashire

Contents

Front cover photograph of Coniston Water by Tom Parker.
Back cover photographs: Top: Penning sheep in Wasdale (Ivor Nicholson); Bottom: Derwentwater (Colin Denwood).

Line drawings in the text are by Janet Acland, Stanley Bond, P. Caldew, E. Gower, J. H. Harper, Edward Jeffrey, A. R. Johnson, Percy Kelly, John Kingdon, P. F. Kingsley, J. M. Marshall, F. S. Sanderson, John Selby and contributors to 'Cumbria' magazine.

Scafell Pinnacle

Introduction

A. G. GARDINER, in an essay written during the darkest days of the 1914-18 war, recalled a vision of Eden that came to him as he stood one night waiting for a bus in blacked-out London. He would take a midnight train and ho! for Keswick. He would see the sun flatter the mountain tops, and set out by the lapping waves of Derwentwater for glorious Sty Head, hearing the murmurs from Glaramara's inmost caves, and scrambling up Great Gable and over by Esk Hause and Scafell and down into the green pastures of Langdale. "And there in that sanctuary, with its starry dome and its encompassing hill, I should find the thing I sought."

The hills and lakes are small by European standards, but they harmonise most delicately. With such rich detail and variety, wrote W.G. Collinwood, "why trouble about the smallness of the picture frame?" The hill assemblages, bonded by cloud or mist, can have swift transitions of mood. Quite often the sky tones are as strong as those of the land. No two days are alike. Many wondrous lighting effects are created as the clouds part and strong light probes the dales or sweeps the lakes.

William Wordsworth, who took the weather of the region in his stride — literally, for he is believed to have covered on foot a total distance of 175,000 miles — wrote: "Insensible must he be who would not congratulate himself upon the bold burst of sunshine, the descending vapours, wandering lights and shadows, and the invigorated torrents and waterfalls, with which broken weather, in a mountainous region, is accomplished."

Imprudent is he, or she, who does not allow for the possibility of rain where the average annual fall is some five feet a year. The rain keeps the becks and falls of the Lake District in lusty voice; it tops up the many meres and tarns and produces a vegetational freshness beyond belief. The Lake District has many sunny days, but there is no more depressing occurrence in this area of light and stony soils than a drought, as you may sometimes notice in spring and early summer.

With a diameter of only 30 miles, the Lake District is England's most astonishing tract of landscape. The frame holds well over 100 lofty hills (here known as "fells") and some 16 sizeable lakes. To list the beauties of the

Lake District is a pointless exercise. Nothing exceeds 3,210 feet, but this region has scarcely a dreary acre. The Lake District takes on a radial form, alternating between dales and fells, with connecting passes, some of them remaining as walkers' routes. It strikes a different note from mile to mile. And fell-walkers usually have their full value — an honest climb to their chosen fell-top from a dale lying only a hundred feet or two above sea level.

Lake District contrasts can be stunning. Wasdale. in the far west, is presided over by the bold pyramidical form of Great Gable which, with Wastwater, is featured on the badge of the Lake District National Park. The near-sterile lake smacks its lips against fan-shaped screes that hold material eroded from the parent fells of Ilgill Head and Whin Rigg.

Yet another Cumbrian lake, Esthwaite Water, west of Windermere, is shallow and serene, with reed beds and communities of waterfowl. Scafell Pike, the highest landmass, is a moonscape of disordered rocks, yet High Street — another Lakeland giant — is fleshed with peat and grass; sheep graze on the skyline.

No two dales are alike in form or character, though all were a product of the same elemental forces, notably the old valley glaciers, which melted some 25,000 years ago. The bared bones of the Lake District were created many millions of years ago, forming three major zones — Skiddaw Slate, Borrowdale Volcanics and Silurian, extending from north to south respectively.

The Pleistocene ice smoothed and tidied them, widening the old river valleys, removing outjutting spurs of rocks, carrying off screes and other debris, plucking out corries. When the old river valleys were scooped into basins, water could gather, dammed by moraines. Thus were formed the lakes we admire today.

Human Settlement

MAN FIRST settled in the lowlands: in Furness, the coastal plain of the north-west, and the vale of Eden. Neolithic man was a regular fellwalker, trudging to lonely places — Pike o'Stickle, Scafell — to acquire rock suitable for making into axes. The native forest was being cleared in the Bronze Age — a time best remembered because then stone circles were reared for a purpose now unknown.

The Lakeland standing stones are among the high fells, for in prehistory high living was obligatory. To seek them out is to taste the wilderness: Banniside at Coniston, Burnmoor near Scafell, Swinside behind Black Combe are good examples. Castlerigg spreads across a smooth hilltop less than two miles from Keswick.

A few Iron Age settlements have been found, and the Romans — arriving about 80 A.D. — found the Lake District as a backwater, inhabited by a few people of Celtic stock. In due course, the Norse element became strong. The period of the Norse settlement in the 10th century has been studied largely in relation to names: fell, dale, gill, beck, tarn, thwaite, garth.

Norse names are to be heard in daily speech; they became the language of topography. Over a period of three centuries, Norse settlers tamed the wilderness and half-filled it with sheep, a preoccupation that continued in

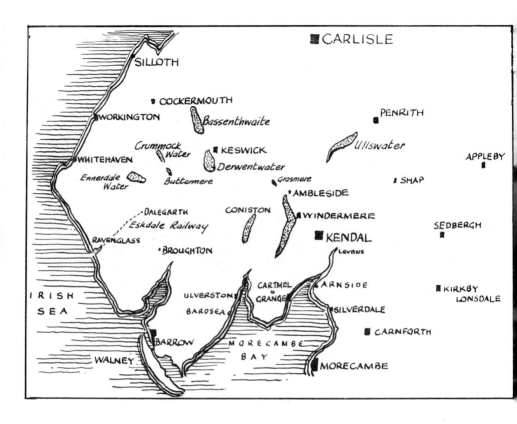

medieval days, when Lakeland saw the rise of the wool trade.

The main centres of population lie at the edge of the Lake District, where the valleys broaden into the low country. Until the transport revolution last century, a dalesman was parochial in his outlook, his vision restricted by the high hills, his gossip coming from the packhorse men, or from chance encounters with friends at the weekly market. He might be born, live, love and die in a single valley, in which his home occupied one end, and the market town lay at the other.

The traditional dalesman had a sheep-like attachment to his heaf. He lived in a square-set home — a type constructed after about 1750 — and in its construction local materials were used to the limit of their value. The farmer lambed his sheep and later made hay in the lowland meadows, which he termed "inland", grazed the fenced-off areas of glacial drift, the "intake", and also ran sheep on the fells.

Wool from the sheep sustained an important industry. Other natural resources were exploited: slate, minerals like lead and copper, and the woodlands of the milder southern valleys which, clear-felled periodically, provided

9

A R JOHNSON —

DERWENTWATER AND SKIDDAW FROM ASHNESS BRIDGE

timber for a variety of industries, from gunpowder production to bobbin manufacture. The industrialisation of the Lake District originally owed its impetus to the power provided by the lusty streams.

With its discovery by the tourist, the Lake District's historic isolation was at an end. The 19th century saw the transformation of the way of life. The Lake District we know today is largely the creation of visitors. Wordsworth was a Cumbrian who returned to the area after years spent well away from it; his poetic friends were truly off-comers. In the wake of the first intrepid tourists, who had the habit of writing about their experiences—and thus commending the Lake District—came the new settlers.

What we see most readily today in the main towns and villages, is a concept of Victorian and Edwardian times. The social life of Lakeland changed quickly and dramatically. Fine new houses appeared beside Windermere; they included a mock castle at Wray. A building boom created houses, hotels looking like palaces and shops catering for visitors. Steam yachts appeared on the major lakes, and steam-hauled trains chugged along lines extending from the peripheral areas to places among the fell ranges.

To the new settlers, among whom — in the latter days — was Hugh Walpole, the Lake District offered escape from areas desecrated by industry. He arrived at Brackenburn, near Keswick, in 1923, and wrote of his "little paradise", with its "running stream, garden, lawn, daffodils, squirrels, music-room, garage, four bedrooms, bath — all. Entranced and excited."

The National Trust, a landowner with some 89,000 acres — or about one-fifth of the area of the National Park — does like to see the old Lakeland life endure at its many farms lying at the heads of the dales. It has some 6,000 acres of woodland beside the great lakes. The National Park maintains a centre at Brockhole, near Windermere, where the essence of Lakeland, its scenery and life, is projected through imaginative displays and lectures.

Sports and Pastimes

HOLIDAYMAKERS in Lakeland are welcome to share in the pleasure of local events. Lakeland folk work hard — and play hard.

Some occupations have emotional highlights you cannot easily forget, an example being the close of a hound trail, when the hounds are in sight, streaking towards the finishing line, and their owners — each with a container holding tit-bits of food — become a waving, yelling, trembling, demented mob. One of the quickest ways of burning up calories is to run across the Lakeland peaks, a sport in which Joss Naylor, a Wasdale sheep-farmer, excels. Joss has actually negotiated 72 peaks in rather more than 21 hours and, apparently uneasy when standing still, he challenged the 250 miles of the Pennine Way, completing it in 3 days, 4 hours and 36 minutes.

If pageantry is to your taste, go to Carlisle for the Great Fair, or to Ambleside, Grasmere or Warcop at the times of the rush-bearings, com-memorating the festive day when rushes laid on the earthen floors of some Lakeland churches were renewed. The Lakeland calendar in summer is heavily scored with details of agricultural shows, sports and galas.

The Cumberland and Westmorland style of wrestling is in a form believed to have been introduced by the Norse settlers. It is certainly popular, with over 60 different meets each year. At some of them world championships are held. A Cumbrian schoolteacher taught this type of wrestling to London boys in Tudor times; the "golden age" of the sport was in the mid-19th century, when the giants were George Steadman, William Richardson, Tom Longmire.

This wrestling style lacks the show-biz image of all-in wrestling. When the two competitors have taken hold and are fairly on their guard, play commences on the word of the referee. With the exception of kicking, the wrestlers are allowed to use every legitimate means to throw each other, and the party breaking his hold loses the fall. There is a dash of glamour in the costumes: pink-tinted or white singlets and underpants, with dark drawers.

A highlight of the sporting calendar in what became known as the "dog months" — the period of late summer and early autumn, between haymaking and the sheep sales — is the sheepdog trial, at which you see dogs working by remote control, exercised by the handler through whistles and shouts. The

11

competitor relies mainly on the whistle, which is clean and straightforward, less emotional than a voice, and carries easily. Guided by its master, the dog moves sheep along a prescribed course leading to a pen.

In hound-trailing, the animals follow a course impregnated with the scent of a special mixture that includes aniseed; it is applied to the ground via some sacking dragged behind the men who are laying the trail. Briefly, the hounds are released to follow the trail, and the first to complete it is the winner. A trail for old dogs must be completed between 25 and 45 minutes of the start; that for puppies between 15 and 25 minutes. If the trail ends outside the times indicated, then it is declared void. The prize money may be shared between all the runners.

A hound in training is walked between seven and eight miles a day, so the owners of hounds may be almost as lish as their charges. A trail hound has a lean body, draped by loose skin; it looks half-starved but usually has better food than its owner. Typical fare for a hound in preparation for a trail is the white of egg and glucose, or several pounds of shin beef.

*   *   *

The Cumbrian Tourist Board, which has a fund of useful information — including a list of coming events — has its offices at Ellerthwaite, Windermere.

Yanwath Hall

The Heart of Lakeland

AMBLESIDE is at the tourist heart of Lakeland. The old town has itself much to offer, and from it roads lead to many stimulating areas. Begin with a visit to the Bridge House, now an information centre run by the National Trust. The building, constructed on a bridge over Stock Beck, is sometimes held to be a venture by a Scotsman to avoid paying ground rent! It was actually built about 1650, when it served as a summer house for the Braithwaites of the Ambleside Hall (which no longer exists), forming a link between the gardens and the rest of the estate.

The old Ambleside church, St. Anne's, was erected on the site of an older place of worship in 1812. You can find it by climbing the hill to the most ancient part of the town. St. Mary's with its imposing spire (it reaches to a height of 180 feet) was built in 1854, nine years before Ambleside was constituted a parish. There are seats for 550 worshippers. St. Mary's has a Wordsworth memorial chapel, created in 1952. It also boasts of a mural dealing with the rushbearing custom, which began in Lake District churches when the earthen floors were sweetened each year by the strewing of rushes. Ambleside's ceremony, one of the four remaining, is held on the Saturday nearest to St. Anne's Day, July 26th.

Of the many walks from Ambleside, you should find time for the (four miles) trip to and from Sweden Bridge, which spans the Scandale Beck as a simple arch, though why it was built is not known, for it was not on an important route. From the centre of the town follow the Kirkstone road, turning left into Sweden Bridge Lane. Those with strong legs can continue from the bridge up Fairfield and on to Helvellyn. A return can be made to Ambleside via Nook End Farm. Half a mile from Ambleside, in Stock Ghyll, is a 76 feet deep force (the old northern term for waterfall). The stream rises on Red Screes (2,541 feet). Approach Stock Ghyll Force by a footpath which begins behind the *Salutation Hotel*. The total fall of water is about 60 feet.

A panoramic view of Windermere can be had from Jenkin Crag, which is reached from Ambleside by Skelgill Lane (turn left half a mile down the road to Waterhead) and through Skelgill Woods. Return distance—about two miles. Troutbeck, which lies two miles from the Crag over the tops, has an

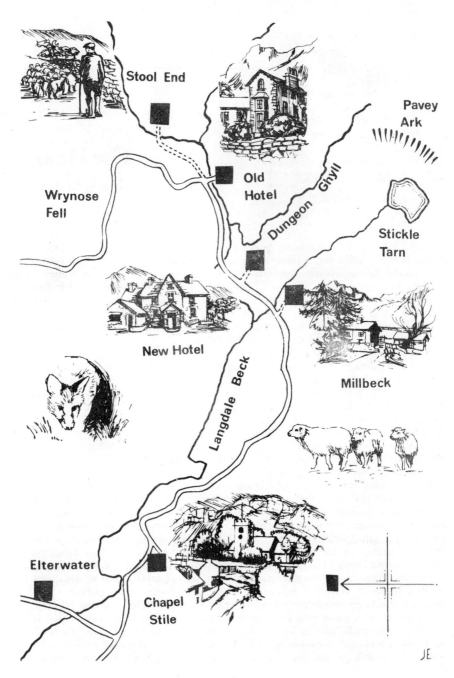

Stool End

Pavey
Ark

Old
Hotel

Dungeon Ghyll

Wrynose
Fell

Stickle
Tarn

New Hotel

Langdale Beck

Millbeck

Elterwater

Chapel
Stile

JE

Great Langdale

Church Hill, Ambleside

old, white-faced farmhouse, formerly the home of the Browne family. Owned by the National Trust, and open to the public, it contains examples of domestic woodwork from many ages.

Loughrigg Fell is a dominant feature of the Ambleside district. It is simple enough to reach the summit plateau, with its tarn, from Clappersgate. Only three miles of walking are involved from Ambleside, and a start might be made near St. Mary's Church, where there is a path to Miller Bridge. Or reach Loughrigg top by walking northwards through park-like country to Pelter Bridge, which is near the main road, and continue to within sight of Rydal Water. The northern slope of Loughrigg Fell is on the left. From the summit a walker can trudge down to Clappersgate, then to Ambleside, to complete the circuit.

In town, the Old Mill is worthy of a visit. A waterwheel is a feature of this ancient building. Standing beside Stock Beck, and of two storeys, the mill includes 15th and 16th century work. There was a reference to a mill here in 1175, and at one time Stock Gill provided power for five mills. Today, the Old Mill is a centre for the production and sale of pottery of all kinds.

The Langdales

WEST OF AMBLESIDE two small dales probe deeply into the mountains. Great and Little Langdale—anciently Langden—lie close together, yet cut off from the sight of each other by Lingmoor Fell (1,410 feet). In Great Langdale the eye ranges across the green fields by the river to where the Pikes stand like two battered Sphinxes. The valley appeals to climbers because of the great selection of rock faces which are near at hand—climbs that are nicely graded from easy to very difficult. The really hard climbs which continually fascinate the experts are White Ghyll, Pavey Ark, Gimmer Cragg, Raven Cragg, Bowfell Buttress—as fascinating a selection of seamed, sheer rock as you will find anywhere in Britain. Little Langdale has a tarn and leads to Wrynose Pass, which crosses the high land to the Duddon Valley. A link road between the two dales lies close to Blea Tarn.

Elterwater, from which you have a first arresting close view of the Langdale Pikes, is really a series of lakes. The name means "swan lake", from the Norse "eltra." Each year it attracts whooper swans, which breed in the Far North and winter in the Lake District. The Langdale Pikes are really Harrison Stickle and Pike o' Stickle, with Loft Crag providing a third local highspot. Four thousand years ago, in Stone Age times, men used a particularly hard local rock for axes, which were roughly fashioned on the heights of Pike o' Stickle, and then finished off in the valleys. Langdale axes were exported to all parts of Britain.

Rydal and Grasmere

THE VILLAGE of Rydal, beside the main Kendal-Keswick road, is small, with just a thin scattering of buildings, but its attractions are many. Here during the latter part of his long life, lived William Wordsworth, Rydal Mount being the fourth and last of his Lake District residences in adult life. Wordsworth's old home is "open to view".

Covering 90 acres, Rydal Water is about 60 feet deep in one spot, though the average depth is only 25 feet. In its water swim pike, perch and trout. Salmon pass through Rydal Water and follow the Rothay to Grasmere Lake. They spawn in the beck near Dunmail Raise. Other salmon, and brown trout from Windermere (Rothay again providing the connection) spawn at the bottom end of Rydal Water. This lake is one of the first stretches of water in the Lake District to freeze over in winter.

Wordsworth bought a sloping field and named it after his daughter, Dora. In the field—known as Rashfield—local folk had been in the habit of collecting rushes, which in those days were strewn on the earthen floors of the Lake District Churches. The property came back to Wordsworth following the unhappy death of Dora, then Mrs Quillinan, in 1847. His grandson, Gordon, handed it over to the National Trust in 1935. Its main feature comes to light in the spring—masses of daffodils and narcissi.

Grasmere, beside a lake in a green bowl surrounded by craggy fells, is inseparably linked with the Wordsworths, whose old home—Dove Cottage—is open to the public, but not on Sundays. It was on a crisp December day in 1799 that William and Dorothy Wordsworth arrived at Grasmere by post chaise from Kendal, settling in Dove Cottage, which was formerly an inn known as *Dove and Olive Bough*. They were greeted by Molly Fisher, who was to be their daily help. Dove Cottage, managed by trustees, and open to the public, attracts visitors from all over the world. The Wordsworths drew water from a well they had dug in the garden. Having eight windows, they paid window tax on two—a shilling a year. The Wordsworths lived here until 1808 and the Poet's old clock is still ticking behind the rough white walls and diamond-paned windows. Across the road, and occupying what was once a barn, is a Wordsworth Museum. Here are objects connected with the Poet, plus a reconstruction of a cottage interior as it was in his day.

Thousands of people congregate in Grasmere on Sports Day, which is held annually on the Thursday nearest to August 20th. The first sports meeting took place in the village in 1852, but in the first part of last century the sports tradition was begun by Professor John Wilson, of Elleray, who started wrestling contests on the shore of Windermere, near the *Ferry Hotel*, and also at Ambleside. Wrestlers gather in large numbers at Grasmere today, wearing traditional costumes (tinted or white singlets and underpants and dark drawers). The Guides races are always exciting.

If you like purpose to your walking, then head for Easedale Tarn (2½ miles from Grasmere) which lies out of sight beyond the dale head, and beyond the spectacular waterfall, which is named Sour Milk Force. You will have about 700 feet of easy climbing to the tarn, which lies just over the 900 feet contour line.

Rydal sheepdog trials

17

Newby Bridge

Windermere

ENGLAND'S largest lake was formed about 15,000 years ago when a glacier occupied an old river valley, grinding it deeper. The maximum depth of Windermere is 219 feet. When the ice melted, water remained in the valley because it had been dammed by a moraine. Today, the rivers Rothay and Brathay pour their water into Windermere at the head of the lake, and the overflow is the lively River Leven. which flows into Morecambe Bay near Greenodd. The length of Windermere is 10½ miles, but the maximum width is only about a mile. A ferry crosses from just south of Bowness to Ferry House (now a centre for freshwater research).

Windermere's largest island, Belle Isle, was once called Longholme. From 1250 it was the seat of the lord of the·manor. When the Phillipsons owned the island there was a siege of eight months during the Civil War, when it was a Royalist stronghold. A Mr English built the present circular house in 1777. The Curwen family became owners a few years later, and the name "Bel Isle"—abbreviation of Isabel Curwen—came into use. (The "Round House" can be visited during the tourist season). A hospital was founded on Lady Holme Island by the de Lindesays in 1256. The Virgin Mary was patron

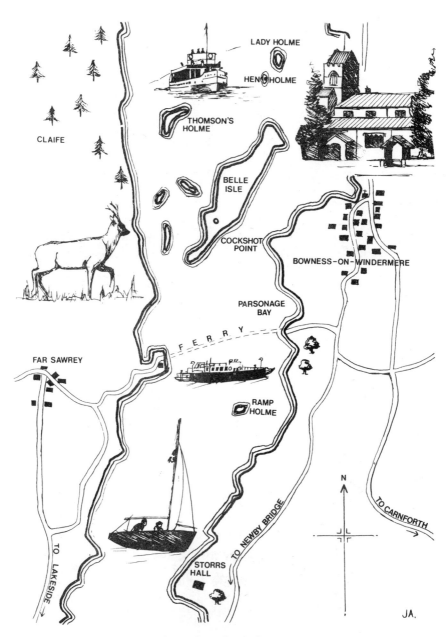

Mid-reaches of Windermere

19

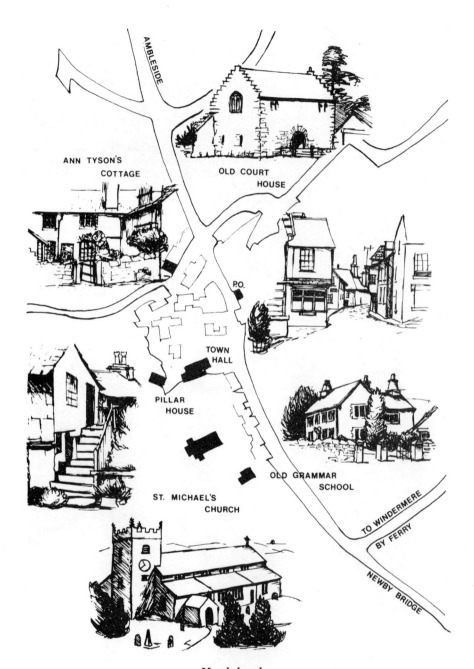

AMBLESIDE

ANN TYSON'S
COTTAGE

OLD COURT
HOUSE

P.O.

TOWN
HALL

PILLAR
HOUSE

OLD GRAMMAR
SCHOOL

ST. MICHAEL'S
CHURCH

TO WINDERMERE
BY FERRY

NEWBY BRIDGE

Hawkshead

of the chantry built at a later date. It became ruined in Henry VIII's time. A promenade was built alongside Bowness Bay in 1912. From it one can see an armada of pleasure craft, a "steam jetty", and Glebe Park, with its putting green, tennis courts, and miniature golf course. There is a large car park just off Glebe Road, and from Glebe Road there is an attractive half mile footpath near the lake shore to Ferry Nab Road.

The well-known fleet of *Sea Link* maintains a summer service on Windermere. Visit the Steamboat Museum near Bowness.

St. Martin's Church, in old Bowness, dates mainly from the 15th century, but it is believed there has been Christian worship hereabouts for about 1,000 years. St. Martin, a Roman officer, who divided his cloak into two parts so that a beggar he met could have clothing, is portrayed by a wooden statue in the cross aisle. It may be 300 years old. The stained glass in the church includes pieces from Cartmel Priory. One piece may date back to 1260, which means that it is among the earliest existing coloured glass in England.

Windermere—the town—was so named after the arrival of the railway. With a mountain indicator located 783 feet above sea level, Orrest Head provides uninterrupted views of Windermere and the Cumbrian mountains. There is a glimpse of Morecambe Bay. (The direct way is immediately north of Windermere, almost opposite the station entrance).

Hawkshead and Esthwaite Water

THIS AREA LIES west of Windermere. The fact that William Wordsworth had some of his early schooling in Hawkshead gives the place added appeal to visitors. It is an extremely quaint town, of white-washed buildings, squares and alleys. Standing on a prominent mound, St. Michael's church literally dominates the village. The roughcasting which once covered the building was stripped away nearly 90 years ago. Notice the Sandys Chapel. Edwin Sandys, a famous Archbishop of York, was born in the parish.

The grammar school is a fine-looking building which was established by Edwin Sandys in 1585, and attended by Wordsworth. During his stay he carved his initials on a desk. Some of his earliest poetic work was associated with this school. Trustees administer the grammar school today, and there is a Wordsworth Museum in the bottom room.

Esthwaite Water has been owned by the Sandys family for centuries. The lake is about two miles long, and at its broadest point the width is half a mile. The outflow of Esthwaite Water, Cunsey Beck, leads into Windermere. The lake contains trout, pike and perch.

Tarn Hows, not far from Hawkshead, are artificial in the sense that they have formed behind a man-made dam. The upstart conifers, though attractive, are not typical of the Lake District. But the combination of water, wood and mountains produces a magnificent picture. In the distance are Red Screes, Fairfield and the Langdale Pikes. The Tarns are owned by the National Trust, which has provided car parks, most of them nicely concealed in woodland. Follow the road from Tarnside and you descend to Monk

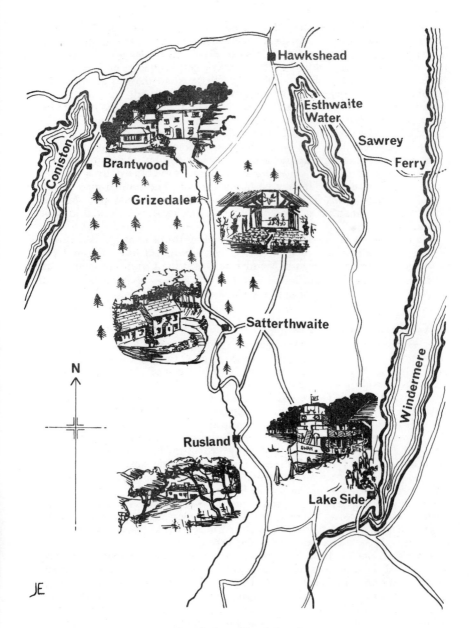

South from Hawkshead

Queen's Square, Hawkshead

Coniston.

At Near Sawrey the Beatrix Potter Museum at Hill Top (National Trust property) is always worth visiting.

Keswick and
Northern Lakeland

FOURTEEN HUNDRED years ago, St. Kentigern was in Carlisle when he heard of the paganism of the folk in the mountain region to the south-west. Turning aside into the forest, he preached and then erected a cross, signifying the faith. The site was Crosthwaite, where the parish church of Keswick now stands. From such beginnings has developed a large community ringed by the great mountains and handy for two sparkling lakes—Derwentwater and Bassenthwaite Lake.

At Keswick, a striking building is the Moot Hall, which dates back to 1571, though rebuilding took place in 1813, using material brought from Lords Island, on Derwentwater. The clock has only one arm. Fitz Park was given by the Hewetson family, and trustees administer it. They also have oversight of the fascinating museum nearby, where you can inspect a rock harmonica (once played before Queen Victoria), geological specimens, local antiquities, and a corner devoted to the manuscripts of Hugh Walpole, author of the *Herries* novels.

Derwentwater, which is about three miles long, averaging only 18 feet in depth, has been described as the "Queen of the English Lakes." It has a special beauty in autumn, when the hundreds of trees round its shores stand proudly with armsful of multi-coloured leaves. Some spectacular views can be obtained of Derwentwater from such points as the Surprise View, just off the road to Watendlath. About three-quarters of the lake shore, including Friars Crag, is owned by the National Trust, which means that it is possible to walk close to the lake.

Crowned by Scots pines, Friars Crag, by Derwentwater, this is one of the most photographed features in the Lake District, but no less compelling for that. In the Middle Ages, Friars embarked here for the short journey to St. Herbert's Island. Owned by the National Trust, it is a memorial to one of its founders, Canon H.D. Rawnsley (1851-1920), one time Vicar of Crosthwaite. Here you can see a Ruskin memorial of Borrowdale stone. Ruskin, who spent his latter years at Brantwood, by Coniston Water, was intensely moved by the view from the Crag looking across Derwentwater to the high mountains around Borrowdale. The view includes Walla Crag and Lodore (to the east), Glaramara and Great End (centre), Maiden Moor and Catbells (west).

24

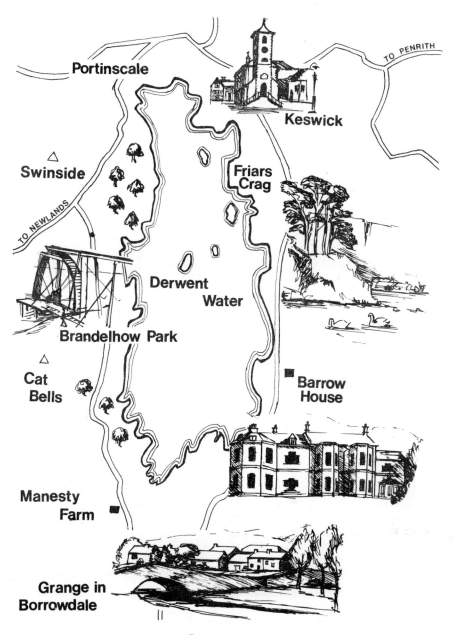

Portinscale

Keswick

TO PENRITH

Swinside

Friars Crag

TO NEWLANDS

Derwent Water

Brandelhow Park

Cat Bells

Barrow House

Manesty Farm

Grange in Borrowdale

Derwentwater

25

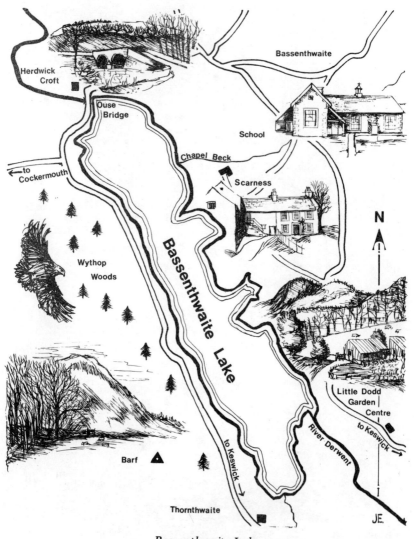

Herdwick Croft

Ouse Bridge

to Cockermouth

Bassenthwaite

School

Chapel Beck

Scarness

Wythop Woods

N

Bassenthwaite Lake

Barf

Little Dodd Garden Centre

to Keswick

River Derwent

to Keswick

Thornthwaite

J.E.

Bassenthwaite Lake

The old home of Hugh Walpole, high above Derwentwater, can be seen on the road between Grange-in-Borrowdale and Keswick, on the west bank of the lake. Walpole lived here from 1924 until 1941.

The three and a half miles from the Borrowdale road to Watendlath provide some of the most memorable Lakeland views. There is tarmac all the way, but it is best to leave the car behind, for from the head of the valley is a pleasant walk across Brund Fell to Rosthwaite, in Borrowdale. The Watendlath road leaves the Borrowdale road at Barrow Landings and climbs 600 feet in little over a mile, crossing Ashness Bridge, from which there is a fine view of Derwentwater, Keswick and Skiddaw. Through Ashness Woods (also Trust owned) the road winds and dips, at one point coming close to the edge of Walla Crag. Here is the Surprise View, the land falling away sheerly to give an uninterrupted view of the lake, the beginnings of Borrowdale, and the mountains beyond Keswick. Watendlath was well known to Hugh Walpole, his *Judith Paris* tale being set here. From here is a half-hour walk to Rosthwaite. The route takes you over the 1,000 feet contour.

Local people are fond of reminding visitors that Bassenthwaite Lake is the only lake in the Lake District. Look carefully at the names of the other stretches of water, and you discover that they have "mere" or "water" in their titles! The lake is four miles long, with an average depth of only 15 feet, but a maximum depth of 75 feet. To journey around the lake by road is

Watendlath

APPLETHWAITE

a matter of 18 miles. Dominating the lake to the east is the Skiddaw Range, and Thornthwaite Forest (owned by the Forestry Commission) is seen on the Western range. Bassenthwaite Lake has the greatest intake of any of the lakes, collecting water from as far away as Scafell Pike.

Skiddaw and its Neighbours

SKIDDAW (3,053 ft.) is linked so closely with Keswick that Southey, who lived in the town for 40 years, spoke of "my neighbour Skiddaw." Only two other English peaks are higher, but although Skiddaw has a most distinctive outline, seen to great advantage from the south, it is less compelling to ramblers and climbers than many a lesser peak in the central area. There is a tourist track to the summit. It is well-used, but the rest of the mountain is little known, except to huntsmen and shepherds.

If you are a moderately good walker you should allow at least two hours to climb Skiddaw, though it has, of course, been climbed in considerably less time. Walk to Keswick railway station and pass under the lines by the tunnel, bearing left for Spooney Green. Here you turn right along Spooney Green Lane, using a route which leads to the foot of Latrigg. The path to Skiddaw is seen after passing through the farthest plantation. The view from Skiddaw in good weather takes in a large part of the Lake District and actually includes the Isle of Man, in the south west. Northwards lies Solway, with that distinctive peak, Criffel, on the Scottish side.

Blencathra—now often referred to as Saddleback—is a broad lump of a mountain. There is a striking glimpse of it from near Thirlmere, where it looms beyond the Vale of St. John. Sprawling over a vast area, Blencathra has plenty of scope for rambling. Those who wish to be bold in an ascent of Blencathra can go straight up from Threlkeld.

Down the four mile long Vale of St. John flows the spare water from

In the Vale of St John

29

Thirlmere, which joins the Greta at Threlkeld. Naddle Fell looms above the valley on the west, and to the east are the northern rocks of the Helvellyn range, with a prominent crag near Legburthwaite called Castle Rock, a mound "with airy turrets crowned," according to Sir Walter Scott.

Thirlmere, once a modest lake of 330 acres, was transformed into a vast reservoir. Manchester obtained its Parliamentary Bill in 1879, and engineers constructed a stone dam which at its greatest height is 104 feet. Today the lake is three and two-thirds miles in length, with a top water level of 587 feet above the level of the sea. The average rainfall is 90 inches.

Helvellyn dominates the eastern skyline, its lower slopes thickly wooded. Beside the churchyard wall at Wythburn is the start of one of the easiest routes to Helvellyn summit. Across Thirlmere from the church a track leads to Watendlath, a 10 mile round trip that should not be lightly undertaken, the route being very boggy in wet weather. Start at Dob Gill, beyond the farmhouses of Stenkin and West Head.

Newlands Vale

VIEWED FROM ABOUT Portinscale (which can be reached from Keswick by a pleasant riverside footpath), the vale of Newlands looks like a great fan, with several small valleys, each with their becks, converging on rich pastoral countryside. The water flows into Bassenthwaite Lake. Across the head of the vale are such Lakeland giants as Robinson (2,317 ft.) and Hindscarth (2,385 ft.).

The best known through route is the Newlands Pass, leading to Buttermere, but the true head of the vale is reached by following Newlands Beck, a task to be undertaken on foot. This quiet countryside echoed to the clamour of copper miners in the reign of Elizabeth I. They were Germans who were given rights to extract the mineral wealth of the area, and spoil heaps and levels remain to remind modern visitors of their industry.

The church lies near Littletown, and across a ford which straddles Keskadale Beck, about half-way up the vale. This is also a point at which there is a fork between that part of the valley leading to Buttermere and the section terminating with Dale Head. White-walled, and most attractive inside, the church was rebuilt in 1843.

Borrowdale

IT IS BELIEVED that the early Britons gave the river its name Derwent ("oak river"). Before 1132 the Norsemen had held this secluded mountain-dominated valley for 200 years, and they called it Borgardale, valley of the fort. Not much is known of their sojourn except that many of the place-names such as "thwaite" and "scale" come from their language. Later the monks of Fountains Abbey were here, having received the dale from Alice de Romille in 1209.

Borrowdale was so remote, so difficult of access, that wheeled vehicles were unknown here as late as the 17th century. Sty Head Pass (name means "ladder"), which leads from the top end of the dale to Wasdale (five miles) was once extensively used for the movement of goods. To travel between the

A. K. JOHNSON

WORDSWORTH HOUSE, COCKERMOUTH, CUMBRIA

two points on a surfaced motor road involves over 90 miles, the route out being over Honister Pass to Buttermere.

As you travel up Borrowdale, look for a disused quarry on the left of the road. A track—actually the old dale road—leads off here marked "Bowder Stone," and indicating that this is National Trust property. The stone, a huge boulder 62 feet long, 36 feet high and weighing about 2,000 tons, has a pleasant woodland setting. Wooden steps lead up to the top. The area is noted for its many birch trees. Borrowdale now divides into two sections, one heading for Stonethwaite and the Langstrath Valley and the other for Seathwaite and the dale head. Rosthwaite is therefore well placed for good walks, including the well trodden path across Brund Fell to Watendlath. Honister Pass begins its high way to Buttermere, and the dale road branches off for Seathwaite. A dozen of the houses at Seatoller were built by the quarry owners when 100 men laboured on Honister Hause. Buttermere, Crummock-water and Loweswater lie in a relatively quiet part of Lakeland and are always worthy of exploration.

Seathwaite is almost at the centre of the Lake District, nine miles from

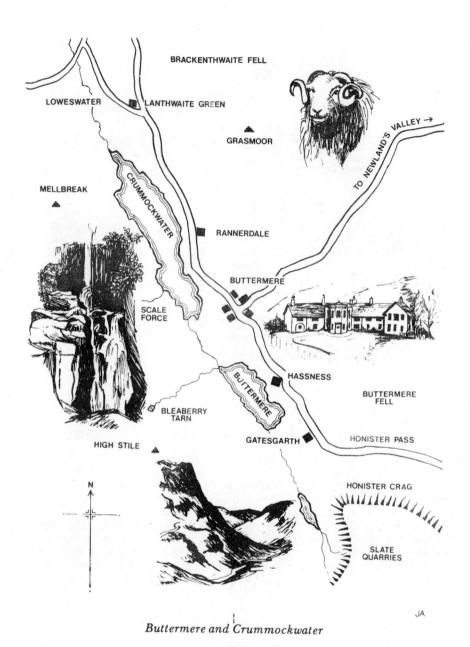

BRACKENTHWAITE FELL

LOWESWATER　LANTHWAITE GREEN

GRASMOOR

TO NEWLAND'S VALLEY →

MELLBREAK

CRUMMOCKWATER

RANNERDALE

BUTTERMERE

SCALE
FORCE

HASSNESS

BUTTERMERE

BUTTERMERE
FELL

BLEABERRY
TARN

HIGH STILE

GATESGARTH

HONISTER PASS

N

HONISTER CRAG

SLATE
QUARRIES

JA

Buttermere and Crummockwater

Keswick. Seathwaite Farm, on which the sun never shines in the depth of winter, and which receives more rain than any other building in the country (about 120 inches a year), is National Trust property. Near Seathwaite is the "wad mine" that made the district nationally known years ago, for here Keswick received its supplies of graphite for pencils.

The highest mountains in England are within easy reach of Seathwaite, though fell-walking should not be undertaken lightly. The commonest fault with visitors to the high places is that they under-estimate the rigours, and another is an unsuitable choice of footwear. Compass knowledge is essential in an area where a familiar landscape can soon be blotted out by mist.

Near the farm at Seathwaite is Sour Milk Gill, where the infant Derwent falls from steep crags. Another waterfall, in Taylor Gill, can be seen just to the right of Sty Head Pass, the summit of which is 1,600 feet, after you have crossed Stockley Bridge, which was once a packhorse bridge, but was widened in 1853. At Sty Head itself you see an attractive tarn and some mountain giants, including Great Gable (2,949 ft.). This peak can be visited from Sty Head Tarn via Aaron Slack and Wind Gap. The pass is your guide to Wasdale.

Buttermere chapel

33

Penrith and Ullswater

PENRITH IS THE north-eastern gateway to the Lake District. This old market town presides over low country between great blocks of fells. It has three rivers: Petterill to the north, Eden to the east and Eamont (joined by the Lowther) to the south. The town's strategic position is best seen from Penrith Beacon, where a stone tower built 250 years ago is sited with views over the Lake District, the Eden Valley, Pennine Range and, far off to the north, the blue hills of Scotland rising beyond the Solway. The beacon was one of 14 in Cumberland; it flared in 1745, when the Scotsmen were approaching. The town had been twice burnt down by Scottish raiders, but this time they filched only a steaming hot pot!

Robert Adam designed two local houses which, together, now form the Town Hall. The Christian religion has visual reminders of a history spanning over a thousand years. In the churchyard are crosses and hogsback stones dating from the tenth century and connected, it is believed, with Owen Caesarius, King of Cumbria from 920 to 937. The church, dedicated to St. Andrew (a name which might help to appease the raiding Scots) has Norman stonework but is most conspicuously georgian.

Penrith Castle, ruined for 400 years, still has plenty of stonework (though old castles were once handy quarries for builders). The castle was a favourite residence of Richard, Duke of Gloucester, who almost certainly inspired its most notable feature; a banqueting hall 50 feet long. What remains of the castle is well-preserved and the grounds round about have been developed as a public park.

Part of the A66 is also the line taken by the Roman road between York and Carlisle. The name Penrith is thought to relate to a ford across the river, and here—only about a mile from town—stood a fort, Brovacum, now literally overshadowed by the redstone castle over which the Clifford family presided. The castle is open to the public. It is wonderfully detached from the modern world now that a new stretch of road has been made and its old bridge does not have to bear the weight of continuous heavy traffic. Lady Anne Clifford, the last of her family to bear the name, was virtually a queen in these parts in the 17th century, and Brougham was her favourite castle; it was

DACRE

here that she died. Where she last saw her mother she erected a pillar as a memorial to the party. For many years it stood at the roadside, now it is seen protruding from an embankment made for the new road.

The principal holiday villages around Ullswater are Patterdale and Glenridding (near the head of the lake) and Pooley Bridge (where Ullswater overflows as the River Eamont).

Ullswater is seven and a half miles long, averaging three quarters of a mile wide, and with a maximum depth (near Howtown) of 205 feet. It has three distinct bends, giving it a dog's leg appearance. The first reach is from the head of the lake, about Glenridding, to Silver Point (so named, perhaps, from the birches which grew here and were regularly felled by clog-makers). Place Fell (2,154 feet) dominates this part of the lake. The second reach extends from Silver Point to Howtown, and again the lake is mountain-dominated, the highspots including High Dod (1,640 feet) and Hallin Fell (1,271 feet). Howtown Bay, a bold indentation in the shoreline, is matched up across the water by the bold promontory of Skelly Nab. The remaining reach has a gentle shoreline, ending with the bold flourish of Dunmallet (775 feet) near Pooley Bridge.

Seven valleys converge on Ullswater, each of them terminating with triangles of low ground extending into the lake like flaps of loose skin. Westerly winds are broken up by the mountains; the blasts, funnelled by the

Place Fell, Ullswater

different valleys, come down to the lake from different angles so that a boatman, setting off from Glenridding in a calm, might encounter a 30 miles an hour wind in the next reach of the lake.

Ullswater has a few small islands, one of which features in old Arthurian legends. Scale House Falls impress voyagers on the lake if the weather has been wet and white water is tumbling down the fellside like milk. Another feature best seen from the water is a simple plaque set on the steep face of a crag to commemorate Norman William Birkett, the champion in the House of Lords over a battle with Manchester Corporation over the right to take water from Ullswater.

Ullswater is clear but deep. A skin-diver who knows it well refers to it "eerie-green". In the depths of the lake, beyond an angler's range with rod and line, a curious fish known as the skelly swims and feeds. Skelly was described as "a sort of fresh water herring" and so little was seen of it in recent years that it was feared to be extinct, poisoned by pollution from lead mines in Glenridding valley. It was common in Wordsworth's day, and he wrote in 1805 that "the fishermen drew their nets ashore and hundreds of fish were leaping in their prison". Happily, the skelly is still present in Ullswater.

Two diesel craft — *Raven* and *Lady of the Lake* — operate a summertime service on Ullswater.

Patterdale

Patterdale means "Patrick's Valley," and Patrick was the early Christian saint. Patterdale is the name of a parish 40 square miles in extent; of a village near the head of Ullswater and of a steep-sided Common north of Grisedale and due east from Helvellyn summit.

The eight bells of St. Patrick's church can be rung by one person, the layout of the ropes being devised so that they are close together and are pulled towards the ringer. Inside the building is a tapestry worked by the late Miss Anne Macbeth; it was admired by Queen Mary. John Mattinson held the curacy of Patterdale for nearly 60 years and his stipend never exceeded £18. He was frugal and industrious and on his death aged 96 he left £1,000. Mattinson had four children and he baptised (and officiated at the weddings of all of them). He also officiated at the burial of his mother, "married" and buried his father, christened his wife and published his own banns of marriage in the church.

Small-time farmers named Mounsey developed a large estate and became known as "Kings of Patterdale". Their home, Patterdale Hall, was referred to as the Palace; the goats they kept on the fells were so wild they could confidently present goats to friends on condition that they were caught by the recipient! Patterdale Hall, home of the "Kings" and later the residence of the Marshalls, has become a centre where schoolboys are trained in outdoor skills like rock-climbing.

Wordsworth would have lived in Patterdale if he had not been terrified by a great storm. He stayed with his sister Dorothy at Broad How and intended to build a house nearby; a storm desolated the area and the couple went off to Grasmere. Goldrill, now a youth hostel, was presented to Thomas Arthur Leonard, founder of the Holiday Fellowship, when he retired in 1931.

Visit the hamlet of Hartsop, near Brotherswater, for the sight of period farms and cottages. Here are two outstanding "spinning galleries".

Helvellyn (3,118 feet) is a much-tramped-over mountain, easily approached from either Patterdale (via Grisedale) or Glenridding. Set out from Patterdale and you can be on the summit in about three and a half hours. Helvellyn's showiest feature is Striding Edge, which appears razor-sharp from a distance. During keen winters many skiers visit Helvellyn's western slopes, Raise and Dodds.

The A592 runs close to the lake between Patterdale and Glenridding, where cafes, shops and hotels are on a tongue of land beside the beck which has taken water from as far away as the tarn beside Sticks Pass and also Red Tarn, Helvellyn. On the promontory, too, is the pier of the Ullswater Steamship Navigation Company. The road returns to the waterside at Stybarrow Crag, whose woodland is now combined with Glencoyne Wood to make up 195 acres of National Trust property. The gem of Glencoynedale is man-made: a 17th century farm which has tall cylindrical chimneys.

The lakeside road has an important junction just short of Aira Point. Here the A5091 branches away to pass through Matterdale to join the A594 (Penrith-Keswick). Matterdale stretches from near Threlkeld to Aira Force. The old Cumbrian farming pattern continues and shepherds' meets are held at Thirlspot and Matterdale in alternate years. The main village is Dockray.

Aira means "the stream with the gravel banks". It rises above Dowthwaite Head, on Matterdale Common, and spills into Ullswater. On the way it makes several impressive leaps from ledges in a wooded glen. The water plunges 60 feet at Aira Force and stone bridges have been built above and below the fall for easy viewing. There is easy car parking, too, in a big space just off the A592 near Matterdale road end.

Gowbarrow ("windy hill"), to the east of Aira beck, is an estate of 700

acres which reaches a height above sea level of 1,578 feet and has a lake frontage of over a mile. Gowbarrow was to De Quincey "that most romantic of parks." It was noted for its red deer and hunting took place here from the time of William Rufus.

Daffodils which flower by the lake are descendants of plants seen by William and Dorothy Wordsworth; they inspired William's best-known poem but it is worth recording that he was also inspired by a prose description of the daffodils penned by his sister. Dorothy recorded in her Journal that the daffodils "seemed as if they verily laughed with the wind."

The National Trust raised £12,800 by public subscription in 1906 and purchased Gowbarrow from Mr. H. C. Howard, whose family had owned it for centuries.

Just before Pooley Bridge the A592 is joined by B5320, which has passed close to Dalemain, one of the most beautiful country houses in Cumberland. It is the property of the Hasell family, who came to Cumberland from Cambridgeshire in 1665. The big house is "open to view". Turn off the B5320 near Dalemain and you can visit Dacre, where a castle—which formerly stood on the Dalemain estate—has now been restored as a private house. It is one of Cumberland's most historic buildings—for long the home of the Dacres and the Howards. Actually, it is mid-way between a fortified pele and a castle proper and it was built in the reign of Edward II (1307-27).

Pooley Bridge (formerly Poolhow, "the hill by the stream") was the venue for the old Ullswater Sports, which began with a regatta on the lake; the last sports were held in 1956. In 1923 Lord Lonsdale brought a party of friends in his famous canary-coloured carriages with postilion-ridden horses. Pooley Bridge, an important catering centre, had a fishing industry and a fish market. The Wordsworths knew the village well; they stayed at Eusemere, a large house designed for Thomas Clarkson who (with Wilberforce) played a leading part in the abolition of the slave trade. The architect was Thomas Wilkinson, a Quaker poet, who lived at The Grotto, Yanwath. Eusemere— like Ullswater—is derived from a personal name, Ulf.

Martindale

POOLEY BRIDGE sees the beginning of a road which extends along the eastern edge of Ullswater to Howtown, beyond which it zig-zags up the Hause, then dips into Martindale. At Dalehead a visitor is only 10 miles from Penrith but in another world—a world of deep-cut valleys, of soaring fells, of remote little sheep farms and red deer. For hereabouts is the only deer-stalking forest in England. Beyond the Hause, the road actually splits into three— rather like tines from an antler of a Martindale red stag. One road goes up the main dale, another probes Boardale and sends the third to the shore of Ullswater at Sandwick (which means "the sandy creek").

About 250 red deer occupy the hills between Haweswater and Ullswater, where they are protected by Dalemain Estate. Most of the deer are hinds and immature beasts. Smaller parties are found much further afield, and these

Glencoyne Farm, near Glenridding

tend to be groups of stags which prefer to live on the periphery of the herd. Nicholson and Burn noted in 1777: "Here is a kind of forest replenished with red and fallow deer." It suggested that Martindale was derived from one of the now-lost mammals, the pine marten, which was then "valuable for its fur." (It is, in fact, from St. Martin).

Martindale is more properly referred to as the Howgrain Valley, which is dominated at its head by the Nab (1,887 feet) and is separated from Boredale by Beda Fell (1,664 feet). Someone likened Beda Fell to a camel. Martindale parish covers 20 square miles and contains about 80 parishioners. The vicarage is at Sandwick. The most modern church, dedicated to St. Peter, stands near the Hause. Much more attractive is 300-year-old Martindale Chapel, just inside Howgrain, which is still occasionally used for services. An appeal for its restoration has been launched.

A mailbus travels from Penrith to Dalehead. It carries mail and paying passengers. Inquiries about the mailbus should be made at Penrith Post Office.

MARTINDALE

The Western Dales

IN THE WEST, three major dales begin among the high fells and open their mouths to the mild breezes sweeping in from the sea. Wasdale, Ennerdale and Eskdale are "unhandy" to most tourists, but each is worthy of being visited.

The most stimulating approach to Wasdale is over one of the passes — Black Sail, the Sty or Burnmoor — but most visitors arrive by car, from Gosforth. In due course they reach Wasdale Head, a grassy arena — Wordsworth's "fertile little plain" — around which are grouped fells such as Yewbarrow, Kirk Fell, Great Gable, Lingmell: bastions of the country of the Borrowdale Volcanics.

There is usually a blue appearance to Wastwater, hinting at its sterility. This lake has a majestic backdrop in the fan-shaped screes. In the middle reach of Wasdale are no lakeside trees, no cultivated land. "All the inhabitants are shepherds," wrote a visitor called Green many years ago. The five farming families of the upper dale still apply themselves enthusiastically to the sheep, which are mainly Herdwicks. This is real sheep country. At Wasdale Head there is continuous talk about tips (males), yows (females) and twinters (young stock). They still hold a Shepherds' Meet at the *Wastwater Hotel*.

Wordsworth compared the pattern of the Wasdale walls to "a large piece of lawless patchwork." The writer Green thought that the dalehead would be improved if the stone walls were removed and the ground more profusely planted. Farmers of long ago used some of the stones they gathered on the land to form walls; they got rid of the excess by forming tall heaps, around which more walls were made.

Wasdale Head's little church is served by the vicar of Gosforth. As recently as 1977, it had no dedication, and so as part of the celebrations on the coming of electricity, a service was held and St. Oswald was given the patronage of church and parish. On that occasion, 75 people packed into a building which can normally accommodate only 50.

The highlight of the social year is Wasdale Head Show, held in October, at which people gather to see hound trails, to watch the fell-runners ascending and descending Kirk Fell, and to observe wrestling in the old Cumberland

Kirk Fell and Great Gable from Piers Ghyll

and Westmorland style.

In the *Wastwater Hotel* are photographs of some of the pioneering rock-climbers; a bar is named after Will Ritson, farmer and inn-keeper, raconteur and teller of stories: a compleat dalesman, in fact, and a trifle larger than life. Many of the photographs taken by the Abraham Brothers—who often arrived at Wasdale on a tricycle—are now owned by the proprietors of the hotel; and a good selection adorns the walls within. The Barn, across the gable end of which the Victorian and Edwardian climbers traversed, testing their skills, still stands.

In the churchyard, which was consecrated in 1901, are the graves of men who challenged the fells and lost their lives. Rock-climbing in Lakeland began in this area. The official history mentions the achievement of John Atkinson, an Ennerdale shepherd, climbing on Pillar Rock in 1826.

Ennerdale Water, to the north, is possibly the least visited of the big Cumbrian lakes. Motorists reach it via Cleator. Even then, no main road goes by the lake, and much of the area has been turned into coniferous plantations by the Forestry Commission. The lake, with a maximum depth of 148 feet, is yet another "static water tank" for urban areas. Yet this valley has its own special beauty, and the people—living away from a major tourist route—are, generally speaking, local people. If you would like to see the old Lakeland way of life at its best, then head to the west!

Eskdale can be approached from central Lakeland over the passes. The Romans knew this route. They built a fort near the head of Windermere, calling it Galava, and made a road over the fells to Eskdale and the fine natural harbour of Ravenglass. Travelling from Ambleside, you will first encounter Wrynose Pass. The Old Three Shires Stone (Cumberland, Westmorland, Lancashire) stands with its feet in damp earth at a height of 1,270 feet above sea level. Yet only Lancashire is mentioned on the old stone!

The road dips to the head of the Duddon Valley, and then takes to the heights again as Hardknott Pass, which slips steeply down into Eskdale and reaches valley level near Brotherilkeld Farm. The actual head of Eskdale is known to a few shepherds and walkers; it lies well above the main valley. The Esk, rising at Esk Hause, 2,490 feet above sea level, loses 1,000 feet of elevation in a mile.

Eskdale is verdant, well-wooded—but lacks a lake. It does have a steam railway, Lile Ratty, coming up from Ravenglass. It is a popular tourist attraction. "Ratty", moving on seven and a-half miles of 15-inch gauge track, was built in the days when iron ore was being brought from a working at the head of the valley; the ore was delivered to the main line station at Ravenglass.

Furness and Cartmel

THE RAILWAY'S COMING to Furness stimulated industry, led to a building boom, turned insignificant villages into quite large communities, created Grange-over-Sands (the suffix was introduced by Canon H.R. Smith, the incumbent from 1858 to 1888) and led in due course to The Retirement Shore, on which every other house is a bungalow. Morecambe Bay is banded by silvery limestone around Arnside and Grange (the town is indeed grey) and by sandstone in parts of Furness (where buildings have an attractive reddish hue).

Green is present in 1,000 shades, from the light greens of the marshes to the dark greens of the woodland foliage. This district is bountifully wooded. The landscape and its settlements look young. The Bay is young. Lively rivers — Winster, Kent, Leven — bring down vast quantities of silt which the restless tides mix with the sand and mud that has already accumulated.

The shoreline now under review extends from just south of Arnside to the tip of Walney Island, where a lighthouse presides over an area of sand and shingle and lagoon. Cumbria's most southerly flourish is on the seemingly endless marshes, which can look depressing in mist but gleam and glow in sunshine, when the drama lacking on thousands of flat green acres is provided by anvil-shaped clouds soaring above.

At high tide, in winter, waders group themselves on Meathop Marsh, near Grange. Curlew, golden plover, lapwing, redshank huddle against the wind. At low tide, the tractor-and-trailer fishermen of Flookburgh move down the old marsh road, thence to the sands, looking for shrimps. The area is low-lying and temperate; when snow cakes the hills the area around the Bay is an arc of green.

At the time of the enclosure acts, in the 18th century, men dreamed of reclaiming Morecambe Bay, and of creating good farm land. It was also thought possible to bring into being a coach road that would be immune from the tides — an idea stressed by a reclamation scheme of the 1780s. Over 1,000 acres were permanently won from the Bay at Ulverston when a ship canal was made; the drainage of adjacent land was necessary.

The Bay remains a playground of tide and river and wind. It is crossed by pedestrians, in organised parties, for the novelty of the thing. Years ago, cross-Bay travel was undertaken seriously. Cartmel and Conishead Priories employed guides for the estuaries, and the best routes were indicated by the placing of small bushes, known as "brobs."

The Abbot of Furness was granted a coroner whose main task was to inquire into drownings. Cartmel Priory received the bodies of over 140 victims of the tide between the 16th and late 19th centuries. When the monasteries were dissolved, the guides continued to function, being retained by the Duchy of Lancaster. Cedric Robinson lives in an ancient house in Cart Lane.

In the 18th century, Milnthorpe was a port for Westmorland, and wharves existed at The Dixies and Sandside. Dallam Tower, completed in 1720, stands in a park tenanted by farm stock and fallow deer. Beetham parish church catered for a big area, and worshippers from Arnside negotiated a limestone crag by The Fairy Steps. The disused railway beside the Kent was formerly used by a regular train known as "Kendal Tommy", after the name of its driver.

Arnside, once a quiet fishing village, is now in part a tourist place and in part a dormitory for business people and a place of retirement. Henry VIII gave the village and the estuary an Admiral, who saw to the safety of the coast and was required to have men and ships available in an emergency. A Directory of 1849 — pre-railway — stated that Arnside Sands "are covered one hour with ships and another with carriages and pedestrians". The railway viaduct, with its 50 piers, is a commanding feature. To secure an adequate foundation, iron tubes were sunk into the sand, which was found to be about 75 feet deep. The first train clattered over the viaduct in 1857. Arnside Knott may be climbed — with ease if you have used the local car park!

The route around the estuary passes close to Levens Hall, an outstanding

The following labels appear on the map:

Whitbarrow

Scars

A590

Sampool Bridge

Levens Hall

R. Gilpin

R. Kent

To Barrow

Ditch

A6

HEVERSHAM

Foulshaw Moss

Ulpha

Old School House

MILNTHORPE

Meathop

SANDSIDE

R. Bela

a swill maker

Dallam Tower

BEETHAM

A6

ARNSIDE

N

Arnside Knott   522

Saltcotes   Farm

Hawes Water

Arnside Tower

JE.

The Kent estuary

47

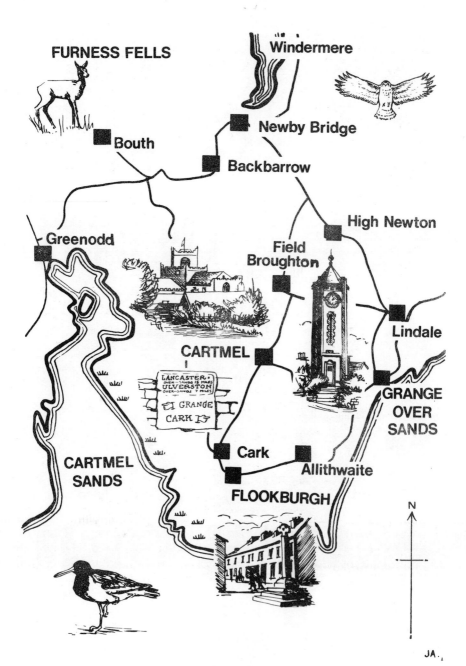

FURNESS FELLS

Windermere

Bouth

Newby Bridge

Backbarrow

High Newton

Greenodd

Field
Broughton

Lindale

CARTMEL

LANCASTER
OVER-SANDS 15 MILES
ULVERSTON
OVER-SANDS 7 MILES
☜ GRANGE
CARK ☞

GRANGE
OVER
SANDS

CARTMEL
SANDS

Cark

Allithwaite

FLOOKBURGH

N

JA.

Cartmel

16th century house that is open to public inspection. It was planned by Sir James Bellingham in 1585, and has been scarcely altered in form since then. It was given a memorable setting when Col. Grahme bought the hall in 1690 and invited Monsieur Beaumont to design the gardens; they are rich in topiary work.

Turnpike trustees built the road from Levens Bridge to Sampool Bridge, the latter crossing the river Gilpin, which flows down the Lyth Valley, an area noted for its damsons. Whitbarrow shows imposing limestone scars to road travellers. The church at Witherslack was built by the Stanley family.

Cartmel parish, which extends over 60 square miles, is almost surrounded by water: Windermere, its outflow the Leven, the Winster and Morecambe Bay. At the end of the 7th century, the King of Northumbria gave the lands of Cartmel, "with all the Britons therein", to St. Cuthbert, and in the reign of King John, the black-habited Canons Regular of St. Augustine were established here under the patronage of William de Mareschal, later Earl of Pembroke.

From the 18th century, it was a "stepping stone" used by students of romantic beauty, from Gilpin to Wordsworth. Cartmel Priory, established in 1188, was dissolved in 1537, but the worshippers were allowed to keep the south aisle of the chancel for their services, and saving an aisle led to the restoration of the whole building by George Preston, of Holker Hall, in 1618. So the walls of the Priory are those that belonged to the original monastery. The extension to the tower is a piece of freak building that was carried out in 1410.

Because the river Ea runs through the centre of Cartmel, the community is

Staveley-in-Cartmel ⤚●

49

is divided between two townships. Notice the signs, set into walls, indicating the distances of Lancaster and Ulverston by the over-sands.

Grange-over-Sands grew remarkably following the arrival of the railway. It has been termed the "Torquay of the North"; the hills come down almost to the shore, and within a short time you can be on the tops. Hampsfell is particularly popular. The ornamental gardens are in an area which, in pre-railway days, was part of the beach. A mile-long promenade is well used by pedestrians.

Humphrey Head (160 ft), near Allithwaite, is one of few sea cliffs along the western coast between North Wales and Scotland. Wraysholme Tower, once a castle, is now a farmhouse, with pele tower adjoining. It was the home of the Harringtons, and Sir Edgar is noted as the slayer of the last wolf in England. More precisely, this part of England! A hermit set up home beside St. Agnes Well, a natural spring.

The sea is a mile from Flookburgh, but local men go fishing—by tractor and trailer. For 200 years, the Cavendish family has been influential in this district. Their stately home is Holker, open to the public.

Backbarrow was a unique industrial site because of its forge, probably the oldest furnace in the country producing pig-iron. Before industrialisation, bloomeries were sited in many parts of the Lake Counties, "bloomery" being a word of Saxon origin, meaning a bar or bloom of iron produced by the direct process. Backbarrow was the setting of the first Cumbrian furnace of orthodox design, built in 1711 by William Rawlinson and partners. John Wilkinson, the Ironmaster, built up his industrial knowledge at this forge by the Leven. The most unexpected of Backbarrow's industries is that producing ultramarine blue; the stonework of the factory is smeared with blue.

Greenodd was widely known as a port, and ships were made here. An early quay was built by Anthony Tissington, of Alfreton, who leased copper and lead mines in the mid-18th century; early in the 19th century a good deal of the slate quarried at Coniston was being shipped from Greenodd. The name Penny Bridge, at the mouth of the Crake, outflow of Coniston Water, is a surname, not the coin.

At Ulverston, you will discover a market town of age and grace. One of its modern claims is to be the birthplace of Stan Laurel, of Laurel and Hardy fame. The "lighthouse" on Hoad Hill is a memorial to Sir John Barrow (1764-1848). He was secretary of the Admiralty for 40 years and founded the Royal Geographical Society.

The coast road from Ulverston to Barrow was constructed by out-of-work miners from Lindal and Ulverston, and by men from the once-busy munitions factories of Barrow. The road is generally close to the Bay. Conishead Priory lies near to Ulverston. Bardsea lies back from the Bay, its houses perched on a hill. The modern road by-passes Aldingham, but you should visit the old church.

The haematite ore country, beginning west of Ulverston, has had its effects on the present and architecture. Iron Age folk may have worked a deposit in the Dalton area; the Furness monks knew quite a lot about it, and Robert the Bruce, as raider, was fascinated by the substance. The Furness ore

Urswick Tarn

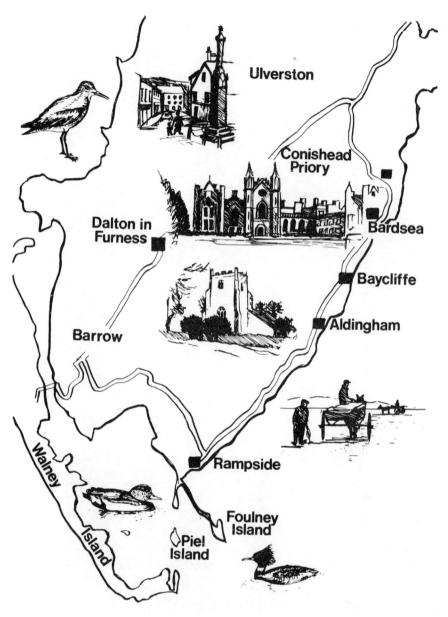

The Furness peninsula

Spark Bridge, near Greenodd

lay in deposits, cradled by limestone, and at its best held 70 per cent of iron. In the heyday of mining, workers came in from Wales and Cornwall; indeed, it was said of the Cornish men that until they arrived in Furness the local people did not know how to talk; they merely "cawed" like a lot of crows!

Charcoal was needed for reducing the ore to metal, and Furness lost its canopy of leaves. Timber was in such short supply towards the end of the 18th century that it was imported, some coming from Norway. Much ore was shipped from small Furness ports to be processed elsewhere. Mining continued until well into this century.

Dalton was the old capital of North Lonsdale when Barrow was an insignificant little coastal village. Furness Abbey, in the Valley of the Deadly Nightshade, is one of the glories of Cumbria.

Barrow grew fantastically during the 19th century. Gladstone, who opened its first dock in 1867, referred to the place as "the youngest child of England's enterprise". It is a bright, friendly place. The main thoroughfare, Abbey Road, is tree-lined. Old civic pride is reflected in the size and scale of its main buildings, and the statues. *Dreadnought*, the first British submarine to be atomic-propelled, was built at Barrow, and so was the *British Admiral*, a 100,000 ton oil tanker. Barrow owed its quick growth to iron and then to ship-building. Yet it is strangely isolated from other industrial centres.

Off Furness are the isles: Walney, Sheep Island, Piel, Roa and Foulney. At South Walney is a huge gullery and the most southerly breeding ground for Eiders in Britain. You may drive to Roa along a causeway, then take a boat to Piel to inspect its ruined castle — and have a pint at the inn!

A corner in Ulverston

Carlisle and the Eden Valley

CARLISLE, as the Gateway to Scotland, was featured on a poster issued by the LMS Railway. The artist, Maurice Greiffenhagon, portrayed a knight in armour who straddled a white charger and held up the flag of St. George. There was also a medieval gateway, complete with portcullis, and a view through the arch of the wild northlands — prettily done, of course, so as not to discourage rail travel. The border city is still romantic, with a top-of-the-map atmosphere that is most uplifting. Rose-red in summer sunlight — for native sandstone and red brick were used for many of its buildings — Carlisle gives the impression of being half as old as time.

Carlisle evolved from a settlement made on a bluff above the Eden. between Petterill and the Caldrew. The railway poster showed one gateway; in fact, there were three set in its medieval walls: the Scottish gate (east), Irish gate (west) and Botchard or English gate (south).

With rapid industrial growth early in the 19th century, the walls were swept away apart from a modest section of the west wall that hints at old-time agoraphobia. Then, in 1974, the new city of Carlisle was created, taking in the former city and county borough and the former Border Rural District. New Carlisle spreads itself over 398 square miles, extending to the Scottish and Northumbrian borders.

It is still a notable rail centre. The station, opened in 1847, was to be used by no less than seven companies, a testimony to its strategic importance. The locomotive liveries are recalled with joy — black for the L. and N.W., blue for the Caledonian, and red for Midland stock; green on the steam engines of the G. and S.W., and a lustrous brown for the N.B.; green for the North Eastern and also for the Maryport and Carlisle, though the shades were sufficiently distinctive to be instantly recognisable. To Carlisle came the great locomotives of the more recent past: "Royal Scot", "The Royal Highlander" and "The North Irishman". From Carlisle went steam trains taking trippers to the Solway coast at Silloth. Progress led to uniformity of appearance, to the closure of lines and the electrification of the Lancaster-Carlisle. Yet Carlisle station still impresses by its Gothic facade, the immensity of its roof, and of the waiting room fireplace, and the coats of arms of the old companies.

Carlisle has few ancient buildings, which is understandable. Yet it manages to impart the flavour of antiquity. The castle, sternly utilitarian, is of the same type of red sandstone that was used, with considerably more artistic effect, in the cathedral — an oddly-shaped cathedral with the stub-end of a nave, some 40 feet long, whereas it once had a length of 140 feet. In that nave, Sir Walter Scott was married to Charlotte Carpenter on Christmas Eve, 1797, and since 1949 the Border Regiment, Cumbria's own, has pondered on its dead. The choir of Carlisle cathedral includes an east window 58 feet high and 32½ feet broad and a ceiling painted blue, with simulated stars.

Sir Robert Smirke designed for Carlisle the two immense round towers of the Citadel and also the Eden bridge. Carlisle Cross marks the city centre, as it has been since Roman times. From the Cross is proclaimed the Carlisle Great Fair, when the place becomes exceedingly "merrie". The Town Hall breaks the ruddy theme in building material. So does the Civic Centre, a modern intruder, of 11 storeys achieving a height of 135 feet.

The "merrie Carlisle" of old ballad-writers may have derived from the number of inns. The city is unusual in that the State has had a monopoly in the brewing and supply of strong drink; it began in 1916, when the largest munitions factory in Europe lay in this area and Demon Drink was pronounced an enemy. Indeed, Lloyd George is reported to have said: "We are fighting Germany, Austria and drink — and the greatest of these deadly enemies is drink."

Inn signs at Carlisle give you highlights of local history. The medieval atmosphere is evoked by the names *Inglewood Forest* and *Robin Hood*.

Cumwhitton, near Carlisle

Carlisle Castle and part of the city wall

Manor House, Melbecks, near Kirkby Stephen

The Border Regiment's victory in the Crimea is commemorated by the *Arroyo Arms*. Carlisle has its *Woolpack, Drover's Rest, Cumberland Wrestlers* and *Two Highland Laddies*. The coming of the railway was marked by inns known as *Royal Scot* and *Caledonian*. The *Museum Inn* was named after a whim of the landlord, who kept pickled snakes and other various curios on the counter!

Vale of Eden

VIEW EDENVALE from the high Pennines, through a rent in the cloud cover, and it is like beholding the Promised Land—so wide, so fertile, so bright does it seem in comparison to the "tops". These are the middle reaches of the vale, to the north of the dog-and-stick country of Mallerstang. Bountiful Eden extends like a fan, open to mild breezes from the Solway.

The Eden lies between the Pennine escarpment—which, visually, can never be ignored—and a high ridge, beyond which are the Lakeland fells. A most powerful glacier took the edges from the landscape and left piles of debris as whaleback drumlins, the best of which lie between Kirkby Stephen and Penrith. The position of the drumlins indicates the line along which the ice moved. It headed to the north.

Glacial drift covers the floor of the vale, but the Vale of Eden has stone of a particularly warm and appealing range of shades—New Red Sandstone, so called to distinguish it from the sandstone of the Devonian period, absent

Market day at Appleby

59

OLD
GRAMMAR
SCHOOL AND
PARISH CHURCH

KIRKBY STEPHEN

from Cumbria. A host of buildings are composed of sandstone whose particles came together after being blown across what was arid desertland, millions of years ago.

The sandstone of the ridge dominated by Penrith Beacon is much harder than those of the vale, where it has made an indifferent building material. At Appleby, sandstone of a particularly bright hue, exposed by the river erosion, has the redness of building brick. When earth-moving machines are brought into Edenvale — as they were in recent times for the construction of the by-pass — they soon acquired a dusty red cosmetic.

Edenvale is large, with big skies. The 68 mile long river has only three towns on its banks — Kirkby Stephen, Appleby, Carlisle — and it can vanish from the sight of casual visitors for many miles at a stretch. Water trickling across the spongy moorland at Black Fell Moss forms streams that are the headwaters of the Eden. Camden wrote of the river's source: "Such a dreary waste and horrid silent wilderness that certain rivulets that creep here are called Hell-becks, rivers of hell."

Extending north to south, Edenvale was the obvious route for Scottish raiders, who dodged the pele towers of Dacre, Dalemain, Yanwath and Brough. When times were more settled, Scots cattle, in large droves, were driven this way, and there were important fairs at Carlisle, Penrith, Appleby and Brough Hill.

Eden today gives its name to the largest district in Cumbria—one that includes Alston and Kirkby Stephen, Tebay and north-eastern Lakeland. The lower Eden is part of Carlisle, and the A66—for long the spine of Edenvale— has lost its importance to the M6, which runs in buccaneering fashion along the higher ground, neatly side-stepping Penrith.

Kirkby Stephen's importance is in relation to the nodal point of five major roads, as a commercial centre for a widespread farming community and, years ago, for the presence of two railway systems, one closed down in 1962, the other—the Midland—being one and a half miles from town.

Brough's importance declined with the coming of the by-pass, before which it had a remarkably high number of catering places for travellers. Nearby Warcop is noted for the Army—and its Rush-bearing.

Appleby, in a loop of the Eden, was the capital of Old Westmorland. It is one of England's most attractive small towns. Its Main Street (Boroughgate) has the church at one end and castle at the other. In the grounds of the castle is a collection of birds and beasts which can be viewed by the public.

PENDRAGON CASTLE AND WILD BOAR FELL

The Empty Quarter

THIS SECTION of our guide covers Shap, the Upper Lune (including the Howgill Fells) and Kendal. The Shap Fells form Lakeland's Empty Quarter. They fascinate the few, but are not spectacular enough for the average tourist. Ice-sheets and valley glaciers, radiating from the High Street area, gouged and smoothed the countryside. Much of it is treeless, lakeless. The Pleistocene chill is still upon it. A quiet landscape, it is the home of a few farmers and gamekeepers. The open ground is tenanted by sheep and the streaky-brown moor birds.

In the area of Shap, the countryside heaves itself to an elevation of almost 2,000 feet, and parts of it are wine-red in late summer, when the heather blooms. Lowther Estates have sporting rights. There are few strong scenic features. John Ruskin recalled: "Ever since I passed Shap Fells when a child, I have had an excessive love for this kind of desolation."

The M6 has stormed Shap Fell, passing — as does the Lancaster to Carlisle railway — to the east of the village. The road-builders had a Wild West sort of life imposed upon them by this bleak, thinly-populated landscape. Just before the railway was built, George Stephenson — who favoured a coastal route — inquired who would be persuaded to travel over Shap, suggesting crows!

The A6, former main route to Scotland, was a road that motorists loved to fear in winter. At Shap Summit, the rain — some 90 inches a year — soon turned to snow; the road levelled out at 1,383 feet. A traveller of 1634 complained that the older route was "no other but climbing and stoney." That was well over a century before a turnpike was made. In the period before the 1914-18 war, the Shap route, little more than a cart track, was shunned by sensible travellers in favour of the routes north through Keswick or Tebay.

The A6 is quiet now. A cyclist told me that it had reverted to the situation he first remembered in the 1920s. Yet before the motorway arrived, using the Lune Gorge to the east, the 14 miles between Kendal and Shap village were among the worst sections of English trunk road to maintain. The route follows no reasonable topographical feature; it has a considerable undulation, going all the time against the "grain" of the

Shap Abbey

countryside. Each winter day there could be about 5,000 vehicles travelling over Shap, with summertime peaks of up to 9,000. A road that, so recently, was among the busiest in Cumbria now affords easy motoring for all.

Gone is the *Jungle Cafe*, and gone the Leyland clock, on its pillar. Gone is one of Cumbria's most remarkable little eating places, the *Fell ·Top Cafe*, consisting of two old buses, parked back to back, with a connecting passage!

The river Lowther springs to life in the hills above Wet Sleddale, in the parish of Shap. There is usually a good head of water. Dr. Burn, author of a local history, wrote that "if any rain is stirring, the air scoops it surprisingly into the hollow of that dale." The Lowther flows beside the ruins of an abbey that gave distinction to this area.

Shap had the only abbey to be built in Westmorland. So tucked away are the buildings, even a high tower built about 1500, that visitors come across the abbey, at the last moment, with a feeling of surprise and delight. Founded by Premonstratensians (white canons), the place had a comparatively uneventful history. Parts of it were excavated in 1864, at which time a local poet, Anthony Whitehead, wrote: "Peur auld Abbey! Some comfort has come i' thy need; Thou's lang been encumber'd wi' rubbish and

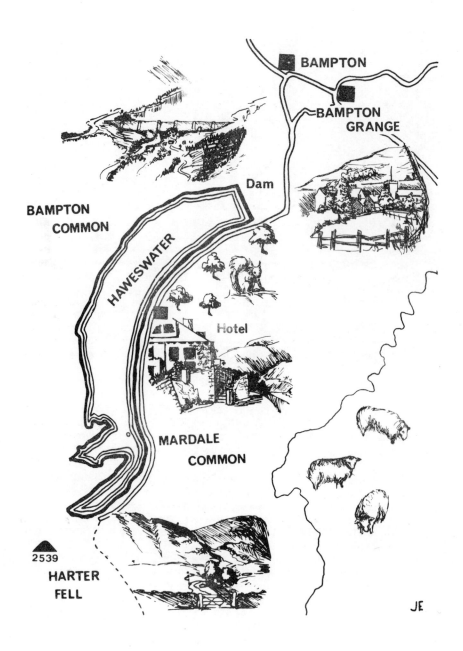

Haweswater

weed". A chapel of 16th century date can be seen at nearby Keld.

South of the village, on the way to Orton, is a group of buildings, with trees to act as "bield", or shelter, that was dedicated to the alleviation of rheumatism and gout. Shap Wells were said to compare favourably with the spas at Harrogate and Gilsland, though a local man described water tasted here as like "train smoke mixed with bad eggs." Around the village of Shap are the famous granite quarries.

Minor features tell of long residence by man. Shap Stones, also known as Karl Lofts, were partly destroyed when the railway was made. Previously, there had been a double avenue ending in a small circle of free-standing stones. With the old forest cover gone, people clustered in the dales that lie side by side, like the partly open fingers of a giant hand: Swindale, Mosedale, Wet Sleddale, Crookdale, Borrowdale, Long Sleddale and — part of the same group, but approached from a road other than the A6 — Kentmere.

Wet Sleddale is well-named, having an average rainfall in excess of 70 inches and a considerable reservoir that sends water through the fell to Haweswater. The dam, gleaming white, and clearly visible from the A6, has a length of 2,000 feet and a maximum height of 70 feet. A track, rutted, stone-littered, passes the reservoir and gains the upper valley.

Wet Sleddale was anciently known as Bannisdale; why — joke apart — it should have the prefix "Wet" is not known. It is, in fact, rather drier than its neighbours, being further to the east, lying just inside the Lake District National Park. Wet Sleddale has an imposing dale head. The main beck rises on Brown How, at about 1,860 feet, and after flowing northwards for a while the beck takes a sudden turn, losing over 300 feet while descending a stairway of black rock in the shadow of raven-haunted scars. For a few hundred yards, the water swirls and tumbles in a gorge linked by rowan.

A 17th century packhorse bridge was dismantled and re-erected higher up the dale, to be clear of the reservoir. An ancient route can be traced between Wet Sleddale and Steps Hall; it connected Kendal and the eastern dales to Appleby, the county town, and is still known as the "assize road."

Swindale, some two and a-half miles long, ends in the formidable crags known as Black Bells. It is now all one farm, though previously there were three. It is an impressive farm: 650 fenced acres, with extensive fell rights. Well over 1,000 Swaledale sheep are at home here. It is drystone wall country, with a considerable variation in the type of rock from one end of the valley to the other.

Bannisdale Beck becomes the river Mint: in the next valley is the Sprint. Viewing the glacial trough of Long Sleddale from the Shap road, a visitor sees a long, straight valley, cut deeply into the fell country, drained by the river Sprint. The immediate view is of a dale that is verdant and lovely, of Silurian rocks but with a series of flat areas on the valley floor where glacial lakes lapped. At the head of Long Sleddale, there is scenic drama with the appearance of volcanic rocks around Sad Ghyll. Those who follow the old Gatesgarth Pass are in the shadow of ponderous fells for the early part of the journey over to Haweswater. Garnett Bridge, seen from the Shap road, is not in the parish of Long Sleddale, which begins with Dale End,

The Upper Lune

WITH THE EXTENSION of the M6 through the Lune Gorge, travellers who had previously gone over Shap found themselves in a stretch of upper Lunesdale dominated by a most distinctive group of fells. The Howgills cover a small area—some 40 square miles. These dome-shaped fells are not exceptionally high—no more than 2,200 feet—yet they demand to be noticed, standing in grand isolation between the Lake District and the Yorkshire Dales. Even in dull light, the Howgills impress by their smooth lines—there is little outcropping rock—and the absence of walls on the upper slopes. In bright light, the unusual shadow pattern hints at something special among hill groupings.

These fells are named after a modest hamlet in the valley of the Lune—a valley lost to the world behind a tree canopy, and approached by way of a road so narrow, and so overswept with vegetation, it is like moving down a green tunnel. The Howgills, haunt of Rough Fell sheep and the lordly buzzard, was Norse country, as indicated by the names for topographical features—beck, gill, dale. All the streams flowing from the Howgills feed the river Lune, which rises on Green Bell, to the north of the Hills. Its course of rather more than 50 miles begins with a westward journey, but soon it is swinging southwards in a gorge with deep, rocky pools in which salmon lie and from which they spring with whirring tails.

Ravenstonedale is at the watershed, but sends much water to swell the Lune, as do Weasdale, Bowderdale and Langdale; their watercourses form a root-like pattern on the maps of the area. Oswald, the North Country saint, is the patron of Ravenstonedale church, in which a three-decker pulpit rises in oaken magnificence, and the pews face inwards, College style. Newbiggin's church has the patronage of a saint equally renowned in the north - Aidan.

Within living memory, road traffic through the Lune Gorge was negligible, but rail services were frequent—and the trains stopped at Tebay. Two branch lines fed the Lancaster-Carlisle system in this area. There was one from Clapham to Lowgill, and another coming in from the north-east via Stainmore and Kirkby Stephen. Following the closure of the station in 1968, and the demolition of buildings, there are just the two main line tracks crossing an expanse of grass and gravel where once stood the station complex.

Work on the Shap bank gave Tebay some distinction among rail centres. It was decreed that no goods train having more than 19 loose-coupled wagons should go up the bank without an engine assisting at the rear. So as a heavy train approached, one of the local tank engines gave a whistle—it was known locally as "giving the crow"—and was admitted to the main line, easing up behind the train to give it a push.

The motorway, as it goes through the Lune Gorge, is part of the M6 that stretches for 230 miles from the Midlands to the Scottish border. Work between Killington and Tebay was spread over 33 months, night and day, in 12 hour shifts. A special access road was constructed, and along it came over 250 items of large plant, including 35-ton trucks. The road crossed the Lune three times on temporary bridges. The old A685 was re-routed along a ledge

66

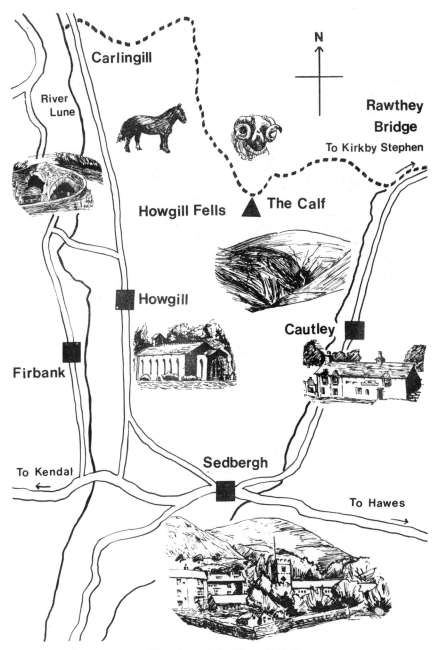

Sedbergh and the Howgill Fells

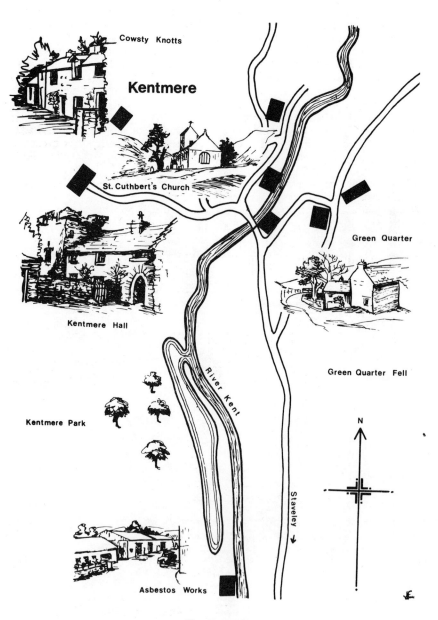

Cowsty Knotts

Kentmere

St. Cuthbert's Church

Green Quarter

Kentmere Hall

Green Quarter Fell

Kentmere Park

River Kent

Staveley →

N

Asbestos Works

Kentmere

68

cut specially from the fellside, and rail traffic was protected by special blasting techniques and the erection of three miles of anti-submarine and nylon mesh netting. Twenty bridges and three major rock cuts were needed, and to construct an interchange on the Tebay flood plain, below the village, over 1m cubic yards of fill were tipped to lift the surface of the new road above the highest-known flood level of a river.

From the motorway, one can see the old Roman camp at Low Borrow Bridge; then the motorway turns, for its direct descent to the Lancashire plain, while Lunesdale regains its unspoilt state. Lowgill, formerly a busy rail junction, has lost its rail tracks but retained its viaduct. Firbank, formerly Firthbank, gives its name to a fell on which George Fox preached for three hours to 1,000 people, a jagged rock becoming known as Fox's Pulpit.

The most important of the towns in this area, Sedbergh, stands not beside the Lune but the Rawthey, an important tributary. Sedbergh, at the foot of Winder, looks across at Baugh Fell, and around it is an intricate network of winding roads. Its local grammar school blossomed into one of the finest public schools in the North.

By the Kent
THE KENT is a fickle river; it floods quickly and declines with equal speed. Owners of mills in the lower valley built a reservoir in a pocket of the high fells to ensure a continuous supply. Kentmere takes its name from a stretch

A corner in Kendal

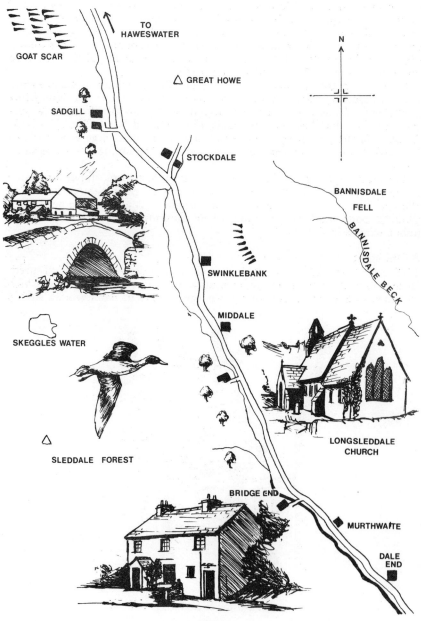

GOAT SCAR

TO
HAWESWATER

△ GREAT HOWE

N

SADGILL

STOCKDALE

BANNISDALE

FELL

BANNISDALE BECK

SWINKLEBANK

MIDDALE

SKEGGLES WATER

LONGSLEDDALE
CHURCH

△

SLEDDALE FOREST

BRIDGE END

MURTHWAITE

DALE
END

Long Sleddale

Kentmere village

of water which, drained by man about 1840, is now represented by a brown smudge on the floor of the valley. A rich deposit of diatomaceous earth was discovered, and a factory was built to exploit it as insulating material.

The church in Kentmere, clad in slate, is perched on a knoll at the head of the plain, and around it are some of the dale's oldest dwellings, also the fells: Rainsborrow, Ill Bell, Froswick, each over 2,300 feet high. A pass leads over to the Troutbeck Valley.

Kendal, by the Kent, is an "auld grey town", light grey in tone, from the native limestone used in the construction of most of the buildings. Four famous old streets, connecting, give Kendal its main traffic artery. Kirkland, Highgate, Stramongate and Stricklandgate enfold between individualistic properties, many of them pubs. A medieval settlement stood at the oldest section, Kirkland.

Speed's map of Kendal, in the middle of the 17th century, shows that the houses then formed a narrow band north and south of the three streets. Areas nearer the river, which are now fully built up, were then only orchards, gardens or fields. It might be said, therefore, that most of the Kendal yards — there were once nearly 100 — came into being during the industrial revolution, and were not built, as popular legend has it, as a form of protection when the Scots were raiding. Kendal was an early home of the woollen industry.

Old Kirkbie in Kentdale was known for years as the Gateway to the Lakes. The gateway became clogged with traffic. Now most of the northbound vehicles use the M6, which lies to the east, or the western by-pass to the Lakes. Kendal, though not in the National Park, holds the Park's administrative office.

Holy Trinity Church impresses by its size. Here is a square tower 80 feet high, and it makes the rest of the huge building look squat. Holy Trinity is 140 feet long by 103 feet wide, with stonework of 13th, 15th and 19th centuries. Within are the chapels of the Parrs, Bellinghams and Stricklands. In 1970, a corona was hung over the high altar in memory of Bernard Gilpin (1517-1583); this native of Kentmere became known as the "Apostle of the North."

Nearby Abbot Hall and the Museum of Lakeland Life are worthy of a visit.

What remains of a castle, birthplace of Katharine Parr, Henry VIII's last wife, straddles a grassy hill to the east of town. Camden, writing in 1586, reported that the castle was "ready to drop down with age." Katharine Parr's "Book of Devotions" is a prized possession of the local council.

View from the Helm, near Kendal

Jaunts to the Coast

CUMBRIA IS WASHED on three sides by the sea. The holiday-making possibilities on the coast are varied, though nowhere are they well-organised. Cumbria does not possess a mini-Blackpool. What it does have are lonely sands and marshes, some huge seabird colonies, prime sea fishing, an ancient castle set in groves of rhododendrons — and villages from which men set off fishing with tractors and trailers.

On Solway shore, Cumbria ends abruptly, just a few feet above the high tidemark, beyond which lies no-man's land: a turmoil of conflicting waters or, at low water, a painted desert. When high tides have the backing of a westerly wind, water ripples over the alluvial flats, flooding stretches of road with such regularity that permanent warning notices are in place. Villages huddle on hummocks above the plain; hedges sprout from grassy banks, and the few trees tilt from the prevailing wind.

Solway is exposed to every wind that blows. A haaf-net fisherman at Bowness says: "She can catch a queer blast." He, wise man, wears three pairs of stockings inside his waders as he begins his walk over sandbank and mudflat to the river in which salmon are moving.

Solway is shallow and looks vast, for the hills stand well clear of the tide's edge. Skiddaw and Criffel (a Scottish hill) keep ancient watch on each other. Sky tones are frequently as strong as those of the land. On stormy days, the sun sets like a raw wound between banks of cloud. Walter Scott, who penned two novels with a Solway setting, wrote of the setting sun showing a ruddy front, like a warrior prepared for defence, over a huge battlemented and turreted wall of crimson and black clouds resembling a Gothic fortress.

A Solway tide moves faster than a man can run; it roars into a rapidly narrowing arm of the sea, surging up the creeks that are like deep finger-marks on the marshes, from which it plucks tons of material, dumping it elsewhere. The tide has the ability to change the arrangement of sandbanks, even the precise course of a river. It brings to light historical evidence such as an ancient forest at Cardurnock, a wooden ship of Viking age off the Eden, and the remains of fish traps off Bowness and in the bed of the Waver. Or so the old men relate ...

The main features of Solway shore are described from west to east. When Maryport and its fellows, the industrialised towns of West Cumberland, flared with industry, Allonby — just to the north — was frequented as a bathing place, and the tradition of catering for visitors continues, with caravan parks, fields containing chalets, and gift shops. Early in the 18th century, a fleet of 50 vessels was maintained here; today, just a few local men make commercial use of the sea. A man with tractor and trawl seeks shrimps in the channels at low tide; another favours the traditional "shoe net", a sandboard some six feet long, with a seven foot pole attached, forming a T shape, and a poke net. Such techniques are possible at Allonby because the Solway current is weak inshore; it strengthens considerably at Dub Mill point, a mile to the north. On the sands of West Beach, between Allonby and Silloth, thousands of trippers converge when summer suns are glowing.

The Silloth we know so well today began life as patches of red on a map dated 1857. The map was prepared when the ground on which the township stands was bought from the Joliffe estate by the North British Railway

Prior House, Abbey Town

74

Company, who laid a track and hewed out a dock to accommodate ships. Excavated earth was dumped round about, and many of today's buildings stand upon it. Silloth grew in an orderly fashion; here is a spacious, well-planned community, with broad streets and fine buildings. The main streets were paved with stone setts; the minor streets with cobbles gathered on the beach.

With so little native stone, builders resorted to brick, which in the first place was produced at Abbeytown, later at works near Carlisle. Christ Church, Silloth, began as heaps of granite, ballast in ships arriving from Ireland. Between Criffel Street and the sea, the land was left green, and clumps of trees, pines, were planted in 1887 at Victoria's Jubilee. Silloth has a fine promenade, extending from Sea View to North House, where it joins the old sea wall. That wall was completed in 1913, the extension—costing well over £150,000—being opened in 1951.

Silloth's dockland is a focal point of interest. The outer dock was opened in 1859 and through it, to an inner dock, come large ships bearing peanut meal from West Africa—meal used in the manufacture of animal feeding stuffs—and about a quarter of all the Irish cattle landed in England; the "lairage" can hold up to 700 head of cattle.

Skinburness, east of Silloth, was a market town and anchorage devastated by the sea in the 13th century; it never recovered its old importance, but local labour built the Sea Dyke, a mile in length. It is related that monks from Holm Cultram were the first to care for the dyke, but in time the Sea Dyke became a parish responsibility. The Long House, by the shore at Skinburness, was featured in Scott's *Redgauntlet* as a meeting place for Jacobites.

Marshland is now the dominating feature of Solway shore. Grassy plains, as level as billiard tables, are stocked with cattle and sheep on a "stint" system, a stint representing the pasturage of a single beast. On Skinburness Marsh, which has 400 stints, one beast is equivalent to a couple of ewes and their followers, or four clean sheep (those without lambs at foot).

Moricambe Bay, from which the road keeps its distance, has a golden glow at low tide. At Drumburgh, a farmstead, formerly a castle, looks venerable, despite its heavy timber shoring. Solway returns to view at Bowness, between the Wampool and the Eden. Hereabouts ended the Roman Wall; the remains are humps in fields, for the wall was used as a quarry by builders. Some Roman masonry was used to build St. Michael's church (from which, in later times, two large bells were stolen by Scotsmen).

The old form of the name was Bulness, said to derive from a bow-shaped ness, on which today you might see haaf-nets lying out to be dried by sunshine and breeze. Haaf is an old Norse word for sea; the method of seeking salmon in a river channel by a hand-held net, was said to be more ancient than effective. Haaf-nets vary a little in composition, but generally have a beam of pine, with legs of greenheart, which is a wood with a "good whip." The net is now invariably made of nylon. Any truncheon-like piece of wood, even part of a bannister, is used as a felling-stick whenever a salmon is caught. Haaf-netting is practised between Bowness and Rockcliffe.

The road to Carlisle unfolds in long, straight stretches in a landscape akin to that of East Anglia. In 1972, the Earl of Lonsdale placed his Solway Commons in the hands of The National Trust for management and conservation, making them a free gift of a long lease of 12 miles of coastal common land, including Burgh Marsh, the foreshore at Bowness, and a continuous strip of coastline from just east of Pasture House round to Anthorn and the salt marsh at Whitrigg.

Port Carlisle, formerly called Fisher's Cross, was constructed for Lord Lonsdale in 1819. A canal was cut between here and Carlisle in 1823, but this navigation was closed in 1854 with the coming of the railway, the tracks being set on the line taken by the canal. Port Carlisle was vacated with the construction of large docks at Silloth.

Burgh-by-Sands (call it Bruff) nestles in low country where the soil is alluvial. The farmers keep dairy cows and grow cereals and roots. The Solway lies one and a-half miles from the village, the intervening ground being occupied by some 1,500 acres of marshland that adjoins the river Eden. The redstone column erected to commemorate Edward I was paid for by an Earl of Lonsdale. To Burgh Marsh, and its even more famous neighbour, Rockcliffe, come the wild geese. By the third week in September, pink-footed geese have arrived in their thousands, to be joined in October by barnacle geese; they settle at Caerlaverock, on the Scottish side, but tend to move to Rockcliffe later in the winter. In autumn, Solway shores hold immense flocks of waders; wigeon ride up the channels with the flow tide. On the coastal mosses are a few red grouse — and adders!

The name Rockcliffe is said to be derived from Raufr Klif, a Norse reference to the red cliffs of the district. It was a busy port in the 18th century, receiving cargoes of timber and Welsh slate. When the river Eden changed its course, the name of a hostelry, *Ship Inn,* became inappropriate. Rockcliffe had an older significance; it was near one of the Eden fords. Today a short distance to the east of Solway Firth, double-carriage road and busy railway provide an effortless link between England and Scotland.

St. Bees to the Duddon

THE FAR WEST has for long been overlooked by tourists, but now it is being lauded by the Tourist Board as: "The Cumbrian Coast: Between the Mountains and the Sea." It was opened up industrially by the railway, but even in 1861 Edwin Waugh was able to lament: "Of all our English lake scenery, no part is less known than that which skirts the sea, from the ruins of Peel in Furness to Whitehaven in Cumberland, and there is none which less deserves neglect."

It is an area of vivid contrast. A visitor to the gullery at Drigg, near Ravenglass, looks across marshland that glows pink from the blossoming of thrift to the shadow-blue fells. Shortly after seeing a ruined castle at Egremont, the traveller looks across the low country to see the futuristic towers of a nuclear power station near Seascale. Man has long inhabited this district. People of the Neolithic period settled by the Ehen, and Ravenglass saw the termination of a Roman road from central Lakeland; a bath-house remains.

Norse immigrants arrived from the nearby Isle of Man, many of them continuing to find living space among the fells. An abbey by the Calder was a cultural oasis in medieval times.

There is an outstanding example to the general rule that the hills stop short of the sea. Old Red-head, as the headland at St. Bees was known, lifts itself to a height of over 200 feet, and the tides encounter the red rock with a resounding thwack. From St. Bees, you may see the loom of Irish lighthouses. This, indeed, was a beacon coast, with fires kindled at St. Bees, Newton Knott above Muncaster and Black Combe. St. Bees has two heads, in fact; the division between them occurs at Flenswick Bay, in which the beach is composed of granulated shingle. The headland is Cumbria's most westerly point.

St. Bees is flamboyant. The red cliffs obtrude between the summer greens of the land and the bluey-greens of a sunlit sea. Cushions of thrift can be seen shimmering in the westerly winds. Bloody cranesbill stains part of the cliff-top in an area where the plant life is of two distinctive types: open country and woodland. The sea cliffs, with their generous ledges, appeal to some 15,000 nesting seabirds. Guillemot, razorbill, kittiwake, herring gull are most prominent at England's third most important seabird station. The auks perch like two-tone skittles on the highest cliffs, near the lighthouse; the headland is, elsewhere, in rather ragged decline.

Looking out to the estuary of the Esk from the main street of Ravenglass

St. Bega — after whom the headland is named — "compelled the sea-mew to furnish her with food from the oceans, while the wolves which then abounded in the district crouched at her sainted feet and ceased to roar, becoming purveyors of sustenance to the pious and solitary virgin." Her life story hints at the strong links existing between the Cumbrian coast, the Isle of Man and Ireland. St. Bees, a large village in a deep valley, is noted for its Norman church and 16th century school. The latter was founded by Archbishop Grindal. The capacious beach, of sand backed by shingle, and large car parks, are well used by summer visitors.

Where an isolated outlier of granite extends to the edge of the sea lies Ravenglass. In this area meet the rivers Irt, Mite and Esk; they merge with the sea in trident-shaped estuary beside which the world is composed largely of sand. Gulls and terns nest on the dunes of Drigg; here, and at Eskmeals to the south of the estuary, a local celebrity is the natterjack toad. Men of all periods have fished for mussels in the hope of finding pearls.

The Roman bath-house, known as Walls House, was used as a dwelling by the Pennington family before they built a pele in the 14th century. In the mid-19th century, Anthony Salvin was commissioned to design a more imposing home, and this he did with a flourish. The pele tower remained, but the extension — complete with a second tower for visual balance — became Muncaster Castle.

The King's Room was actually built and dedicated to him by name long after Henry VI, flying from the battle of Hexham, found temporary refuge at Muncaster; he gave the family a bowl of greenish glass, the Luck of Muncaster, which endures. Muncaster, which is "open to view" attracts people in spring because of its massed rhododendrons and azaleas. A terrace of grass, with clipped hedges, overlooks a sweep of the Esk valley.

Low Nest Farm, near Keswick

Reference
Section

Where to go - wet or fine
Things to do
What's on

Outdoor Lakeland

(including the surrounding areas of Cumbria)

Places of Historic Interest

AMBLESIDE Roman Fort: Situated in Borrans Park alongside the road leading from Waterhead to Skelwith Bridge. Known as Galava in Roman times, the remains of the fort are now under the custody of the National Trust.

APPLEBY Castle: 11th century Norman keep with surrounding medieval buildings. For details of conservation centre see 'Country Parks and Nature Trails'. Daily, beginning of May to end of September, 10.30am - 5.0pm; also at Easter.

BARROW—Furness Abbey: One of the finest monastic ruins in the country. The remains, in distinctive red sandstone, include dormitories, cloisters and refectory. Situated just off the main A590 road on the approach to Barrow from Dalton. Department of the Environment property.

BARROW—Piel Castle: Ruins on Piel Island of a characteristic Norman motte and bailey castle which was later used by the monks of Furness Abbey. Access is by boat from Roa Island (reached from Rampside by a connecting causeway).

BEWCASTLE Cross: In a remote part of northern Cumbria. From Brampton take the A6071 Longtown road, and after about 1½ miles turn right for Walton and Nickies Hill where join the B6318. Turn right and in one mile left—then follow signs to Bewcastle. The magnificent 14ft high cross was built in the latter half of the 7th century and features some superb carvings of the period.

BRAMPTON—Lanercost Priory: North of the town close to the river Irthing. Augustinian house dating from 1166; the north aisle of the original church now forms the parish church and is surrounded by the ruins of the other buildings. DoE property. Daily, April to September, 9.30am—7.0pm; also October to March, Saturdays 9.30am—5.30pm and Sundays 2.0pm - 5.30pm (4.0pm November - February).

BROUGH Castle: Norman keep with 13th and 14th century domestic buildings; restored by Lady Anne Clifford in 17th century. DoE property. Open mid-March to mid-October.

BROUGHTON-IN-FURNESS—Swinside Stone Circle: Lies to the south-west of the fell road connecting Broughton with Ravenglass. Access by bridleways. The circle is 90 feet across and consists of 55 stones.

BURTON—Dalton deserted village: One of the best preserved deserted medieval villages in the country. To the south-east of Burton which is on the A6070 road from Crooklands to Carnforth. Access is over a stile on the left of a private road leading to Dalton Old Hall.

CARLISLE Castle: 12th century keep and 13th century gatehouse with portcullis, half-moon battery and ramparts. For details of the Regimental Museum see 'Museums and Art Centres'. Weekdays 9.30am - 6.30pm (4.0pm mid-October to mid-March); Sundays 2.0pm - 6.30pm (4.0pm mid-October to mid-March). Also open Sunday mornings, May to September.

EGREMONT Castle: Early Norman site with ruins of 12th century castle. In public park—open all year.

ESKDALE—Hardknott Castle: Impressively situated Roman fort half-way down Hardknott Pass. Covers three acres and includes a three-room bath house and a parade ground.

GOSFORTH Cross: Stands in the churchyard near the lych-gate. Slender shaft about 15ft high and believed to be the tallest cross in Britain. Probably carved by the Vikings in the 10th century, each face depicts part of a Norse poem. Gosforth is on the A595 coast road between Ravenglass and Egremont.

HADRIAN'S WALL: The most spectacular Roman relic in Britain running for 73 miles across the width of northern England from Wallsend, near Newcastle, to Bowness-on-Solway. There are several important remains in Cumbria north-east of Brampton between Lanercost and Gilsland. These include Banks Burn, a fine stretch of the wall; Turret 52a, originally a turf wall structure; and Birdoswald Fort which housed an 800-strong infantry cohort. It is well worth venturing into Northumberland to visit the central sector of the wall where the best preserved remains are situated —for example, Great Chesters (fort); Winshields Crags (a fine section close to the highest point of the wall); Housesteads (the most impressive of the remaining forts with ramparts, gateways, granaries, latrines, etc, plainly visible); and Carrawburgh (contains a modern reconstruction of part of a Temple of Mithras).

KENDAL Castle: Ruins of 12th century castle, famed as the home of Katherine Parr, the sixth wife of Henry VIII. Situated in public park.

KESWICK—Castlerigg Stone Circle: Two miles east of the town by the side of the old Penrith road. Maximum diameter of 107 feet and comprising 38 huge boulders with ten additional stones forming an eastern inner sanctuary. Late Neolithic or Bronze Age date.

KIRKBY STEPHEN—Pendragon Castle: South of the town alongside the B6259 road through Mallerstang. Remains of 12th century castle restored by Lady Anne Clifford. Reputedly the home of Uther Pendragon, the father of King Arthur. No access to ruins but visible from road.

KIRKOSWALD Castle: Remains of 13th century castle and 15th century moat on high ground offering extensive views. South-east of the village off the B6413 Plumpton - Brampton road.

PENRITH—Brougham Castle: Alongside the A66 road at the point where it crosses the river Eamont. One of the most fascinating castle ruins in northern England, it is situated on the site of the Roman fort of Brocavum which guarded the Stainmore road. 12th century keep, later restored by Lady Anne Clifford. Opening hours as Carlisle Castle.

PENRITH Castle: 14th century defence against Scottish raids, inhabited by Warwick the King-maker and the Duke of Gloucester, later Richard III. Situated in a public park—free admission.

PENRITH—Long Meg and her Daughters: Near Little Salkeld, north of the A686 Penrith to Alston road. The second largest stone circle in England (after Stonehenge), it is 400 yards in circumference and contains 59 stones in all. Long Meg herself stands alone and is some 18ft high.

RAVENGLASS—Walls Castle: Well preserved bath house of the Roman fort of Glannaventa. The walls stand to almost 13ft high and include several almost complete archways as well as traces of the hypocaust which supplied heat to the various rooms.

SHAP Abbey: Completely hidden in a fold of the hills, the ruins of this 12th century Premon-stratensian foundation are dominated by a 16th century tower extending almost to its original height. The abbey is reached by taking the Bampton road in Shap village.

Gardens

AMBLESIDE—Rydal Mount: The 4½ acre garden was landscaped by William Wordsworth. With its two long terraces and numerous rare trees and shrubs, it is widely regarded as one of the most imteresting small gardens in England. For opening hours see 'Historic Houses'.

AMBLESIDE—Stagshaw: Woodland garden on a steep slope overlooking Windermere, ½ mile south of Ambleside on A591. Unique collection of azaleas, camellias and rhododendrons. Daily, 10.0am - 7.30pm or sunset if earlier.

CARLISLE—Corby Castle: At Great Corby, off the A69 Carlisle to Newcastle road. The grounds, laid out by Thomas Howard in the 18th century, include a cascade tempietta and a riverside walk of almost a mile. Open daily.

CARNFORTH—Leighton Hall: A mile to the west of the A6 through the village of Yealand Conyers. Woodland walk and extensive gardens. For opening hours see 'Historic Houses'.

HOLKER Hall: The formal and woodland gardens are famous for their flowers and especially for the rhododendrons. For opening hours see 'Historic Houses'.

KESWICK—Lingholm Gardens: Alongside Derwentwater, reached off the minor road connecting Portinscale with Grange-in-Borrowdale. Extensive woodland and formal gardens giving splendid views. Daily, April to October, 10.0am - 5.0pm.

KIRKOSWALD—Nunnery Walks: The walks commence at Armathwaite Nunnery, a house at Staffield on the Kirkoswald to Armathwaite road, and include some spectacular waterfalls. The route is not suitable for very young children or elderly people and great care should be taken during or after wet weather when it can be very slippery.

LEVENS Hall: The famous topiary gardens were laid out in 1692 by a pupil of Le Notre. There is a plant centre. Daily, 10.0am - 5.0pm except winter weekends.

NEWBY BRIDGE—Graythwaite Hall: 3½ miles to the north on the road to Hawkshead. Seven acres of landscaped gardens with rhododendrons, azaleas and other shrubs. Beginning of April to end of June, daily, 10.0am - 6.0pm.

RAVENGLASS—Muncaster Castle: The rhododendron garden is famous throughout Europe. There is also a bird garden. Ruskin's 'Gateway to Paradise' offers superb views over Eskdale. Easter to beginning of October, daily (except Fridays) 12.0 noon - 5.0pm.

TEMPLE SOWERBY—Acorn Bank: Off A66 between Penrith and Appleby. Walled garden with spring bulbs, herbaceous plants and herbs. National Trust property. April to end of October, daily (except Mondays) 10.0am - 5.30pm.

WINDERMERE—Belle Isle: This 30 acre island includes a rhododendron walk and a rose garden. Admission is by boat from Bowness. For opening hours see 'Historic Houses'.

WINDERMERE—Holehird: Lakeland Horticultural Society's garden just off the A592 Penrith road north-east of Troutbeck Bridge. Specimen trees, rock gardens, displays of flowering shrubs. Fine views over Windermere; open at all reasonable hours.

Country Parks and Nature Trails

AMBLESIDE—Loughrigg Fell: Start from Bridge House, Ambleside. Open fell pasture and riverside path with some mixed woodland. Guide from National Trust and National Park information centres. 2½ miles.

AMBLESIDE—White Moss Common: Start is north of Rydal off A591 Grasmere road. Fell and mixed woodland with interesting geological features. Guide from National Trust and National Park information centres. 1 mile.

APPLEBY—Appleby Castle Conservation Centre: Rare species and survival centre including threatened breeds of farm animals as well as owls, pheasants, ravens and waterfowl. Car park, shop, tea room and picnic areas. There is a nature trail of 1½ miles or less—guide from castle entrance. Daily, beginning of May to end of September (also Easter), 10.30am - 5.0pm.

APPLEBY—Holme Wood Woodland Trail: Alongside river Eden, 200 yards downstream from A66. Woodland with many species of trees and birds. June to mid-October; guide from Tourist Information Centre, Appleby. ½ mile.

ARNSIDE—Arnside Knott: Start at Sauls Drive, one mile south-west of Arnside. Guide from local shops and National Trust information centres. Two trails--allow respectively ¾ hour and 2 hours.

BASSENTHWAITE—Dodd Wood Forest Trail and Walks: Begin from car park and picnic site at Skill Beck, four miles north of Keswick on A591 Carlisle road. There is a trail of 1½ miles, short walk of a few hundred yards and a long walk of 3 miles to the 1,612ft summit of Dodd. Guide available at car park or nearest Tourist Information Centre. Daily, Easter to October.

BORROWDALE—Johnny Wood: Start from car park at Seatoller. Attractive mixture of oak forest, woodland and open fell with good views. Guide from National Trust and National Park information centres. 2 or 2½ miles.

BRAMPTON—Talkin Tarn Country Park: South of the town just off the B6413 Castle Carrock road. Includes the tarn itself and a large area of woodland. Rowing boats for hire; sailing; fishing; canoeing; camping. Open throughout the year.

CARLISLE—Eden Riverside Trail: Runs alongside the river from Eden Bridge to woodland at Willow Holme and includes remains of Hadrian's Wall. Guide from Carlisle Tourist Information Centre. Up to 3¾ miles.

CARLISLE—Kingmoor Nature Trail: Woodland walk off Kingmoor Road, 1½ miles north of city centre. Guide from Carlisle Tourist Information Centre. 1 or 2½ miles.

CARNFORTH—Leighton Hall: To the west of the A6 through the village of Yealand Conyers. The grounds include a nature trail. Birds of prey are flown in unique displays every open afternoon starting at 3.30pm. For opening hours see 'Historic Houses'.

CONISTON—Brantwood: Variety of oakwood with waterfalls and interesting plant and animal life. Information centre open daily (except Saturdays), Easter to end of October, 11.0am - 5.30pm. 3½ miles in three consecutive sections.

ENNERDALE—Nine Becks: Guide from box at car park at Bowness Point mid-way along northern side of Ennerdale Water. 9 miles.

ENNERDALE—Smithy Beck: Overlooking northern side of Ennerdale Water. Guide from box at Bowness Point car park. Allow between one and two hours.

ESKDALE—Stanley Ghyll: On the south side of Eskdale opposite Boot. Guide from National Park information centres. 2 miles.

GRANGE-OVER-SANDS— Hampsfell Nature Trail: Start is on the west side of the B5271 Grange - High Newton road. Mixture of woods, grassland and limestone pavement. Guide from Grange Tourist Information Centre. Allow 2 to 3 hours.

GRIZEDALE FOREST—Bogle Crag: Waymarked forest walks of varying lengths. Picnic site and car park.

GRIZEDALE FOREST—Millwood Trail: Start from Visitor & Wildlife Centre (guide available). 1 mile.

GRIZEDALE FOREST—Silurian Way: Waymarked walk around the forest designed to show all aspects of forestry operations. Start from Visitor & Wildlife Centre (guide available). 9½ miles.

KENDAL—Kendal Canal Nature Trail: Start from Field End Bridge, near Stainton, five miles south of Kendal off A65. Short trail alongside disused Lancaster Canal. Guide from Kendal Museum, Brewery Arts Centre, etc.

KENDAL—Serpentine Woods Nature Trail: On the north-west side of the town 200 yards up Serpentine Road. Woods and open fell. 1 mile.

KESWICK—Friar's Crag: Start from car park at Derwentwater boat landings. Woodland and lakeshore with good views. Guide from National Trust and National Park information centres. 1½ miles.

NEWBY BRIDGE—Fell Foot Country Park: 18 acre park with lake frontage at southern end of Windermere, alongside A592 Newby Bridge to Bowness road. Boat hire facilities, fishing, picnic areas, cafe and information centre. National Trust property.

PENRITH—Lowther Wildlife Park: Situated just off the A6, four miles south of Penrith. Visitors can drive through over 100 acres of parkland on specially constructed roads. The rich variety of wildlife includes deer, otters, badgers, wild cats, wolves and flamingos. Shop and self-service cafeteria. Easter to October, 10.0am - 5.0 pm.

RAVENGLASS—Muncaster: Nature trail of 2 miles and tree trail of 1½ miles. Guide available at starting point.

SAWREY—Claife Nature Walk: On west shore of Windermere close to the ferry. Includes mixed woodland and lakeshore walk. Guide from National Trust and National Park information centres. 1½ miles.

SILVERDALE—Eaves Wood: Woodland on limestone pavement giving superb views over Morecambe Bay. Guide from local newsagent. 2 miles.

THIRLMERE—Launchy Ghyll Forest Trail: Starts halfway along western shore of lake. Guide from box at starting point. 1 mile.

THIRLMERE—Swirls Forest Trail: Start from gate on east side of A591 midway along lake. Circular route through coniferous forest. Guide from box at starting point. 1 mile.

ULVERSTON—Bardsea Country Park: Off the A5087 Ulverston to Barrow coast road. 85 acre park with seashore, coastline walk, woodland and picnic facilities.

WASDALE—Nether Wasdale Nature Trail: Close to the lower reaches of Wastwater. Guide from National Trust and National Park information centres. 1½ miles.

WHINLATTER PASS—Whinlatter Forest Trail: Start from the Visitor Centre which includes car parks with picnic areas and tables. Forest map from Visitor Centre. 1½ miles (with shorter alternatives).

WINDERMERE—Belle Isle Nature Trail: Trail round part of this 30 acre island. Access by boat from Bowness. Guide from shop at the house—for opening hours see 'Historic Houses'.

WINDERMERE—Brockhole: The grounds of Brockhole (see 'Visitor Centres') include picnic facilities, mixed woodland and a lakeside walk offering fine views over Windermere. There is also a ½ mile nature trail—guide available at starting point. Daily, end of March to end of October.

Nature Reserves

ARNSIDE—Beach Wood: Over an acre of meadow and mixed woodland on shore of Kent estuary. Nesting and sea birds. Unrestricted access.

BARROW-IN-FURNESS—South Walney: At the southern end of Walney Island. Noted for its summer population of gulls and eider duck and in winter as a migration area for ducks and waders. Day permits available. Open daily (except Mondays) from 10.0am.

GLASSON Moss: Large area of sphagnum bog and rare mosses off the road linking Carlisle with Bowness-on-Solway. Unrestricted access.

SILVERDALE—Leighton Moss: Nationally known R.S.P.B. reserve between Carnforth and Silverdale. Noted for its breeding bitterns and reed warblers and many other rare birds. Open on Wednesdays, Thursdays, Saturdays and Sundays (Wednesdays and Sundays only in winter). Permits available on arrival.

WHITEHAVEN—St Bees Head: Breeding ground of guillemots, kittiwakes, puffins, razorbills, etc. The public footpath along the clifftop, two miles south of Whitehaven, has signposted observation points.

Town Trails

APPLEBY: Walk around the Norman area of the town. Guide from Appleby Tourist Information Centre. 1½ miles.

BARROW-IN-FURNESS—Biggar: Trail round the cobble-built houses of this village on Walney Island. Guide from Barrow Tourist Information Centre. ¼ mile.

BARROW-IN-FURNESS — Furness Abbey: Guide from Barrow Tourist Information Centre. 3 miles.

BARROW-IN-FURNESS—Vickerstown: Trail round the settlement on Walney Island built at the turn of the century to house the workforce of Vickers Ltd. Guide from Barrow Tourist Information Centre. ¾ mile.

BARROW-IN-FURNESS—Town Centre: Takes in examples of the Victorian architecture in this town which was created by the Furness Railway company. Guide from Barrow Tourist Information Centre. 1¼ miles.

CARLISLE: Includes the cathedral, city walls and 14th century Guildhall. Guide from Carlisle Tourist Information Centre. 1 mile.

COCKERMOUTH: A walk around the town. Guide from Cockermouth Tourist Information Centre and local bookshops. 4 miles or shorter.

DALTON-IN-FURNESS: A town trail which includes the castle and several Georgian houses. Guide from Barrow Tourist Information Centre. 1½ miles.

KENDAL: Includes both ancient and modern buildings in the town. Guide from Kendal Tourist Information Centre and local bookshops. 1½ miles.

KIRKBY LONSDALE: A walk extending from the church to Devil's Bridge and embracing many intervening features. Picture map and tour route from local shops. 1 mile.

LINDAL-IN-FURNESS: Interesting tour of this village and its associations with the 19th century iron ore industry. Guide from Barrow Tourist Information Centre. 1½ miles.

MARYPORT: Two walks around the town and the harbour. Guide from Maryport Tourist Information Centre. Allow 1½ hours and 2 hours.

SEDBERGH: Guide from Yorkshire Dales National Park Information Centre. 1 mile.

WHITEHAVEN: A walkabout through this historic town. Guide from Whitehaven Tourist Information Centre. 1 mile (plus detours).

Guided Walks

The Lake District National Park runs a comprehensive programme of guided walks each season. There are also special 'Discovery Walks' for which a charge is made and booking is advisable. Walkers are advised to wear boots or stout shoes and windproof clothing. Walks start from the following centres (1981):- Ambleside; Bowness Bay; Buttermere; Coniston; Elterwater; Grasmere; Hawkshead; Keswick; Pooley Bridge; Ravenglass; Seatoller; Skelwith Bridge; Ullswater; Windermere. Full details are available from National Park Information Centres.

At Carlisle there is a guided walk most evenings in the season, starting from the Crown & Mitre Hotel and taking in the cathedral, castle and city walls.

Grass Skiing

WINDERMERE—International Grass Ski Centre: In Limefitt Park; open summer months only. Instruction; nursery and graded slopes; ski equipment and boot hire; ski lift.

Riding

A considerable number of establishments offer facilities for riding, riding instruction, pony trekking or trail riding. The details below are subject to change and should be checked with local information centres.

CENTRAL LAKELAND

Craig Level Riding School, Lake Road, Windermere. Tel Windermere 3572.
Limefitt Park, Windermere. Tel Ambleside 2564.
Sawrey Knotts Hotel, Far Sawrey. Tel Windermere 2105.
Spoon Hall, Coniston. Tel Coniston 391.
Tarn Hows Hotel, Hawkshead. Tel Hawkshead 330.
Wynlass Beck, Windermere. Tel Windermere 3811.

NORTHERN LAKELAND

Hill Farm, Bassenthwaite. Tel Bassenthwaite Lake 498.
Robin Hood Riding & Trekking Centre, Bassenthwaite. Tel Bassenthwaite Lake 296.
Setmabanning Farm, Threlkeld, Keswick. Tel Threlkeld 229.
Town End Trekking Centre, Haltcliffe, Hesket Newmarket. Tel Caldbeck 638.
Windebrowe Riding Centre, Keswick. Tel Keswick 72706.

PENRITH AND ULLSWATER

Ellerslea Trekking Centre, Pooley Bridge. Tel Pooley Bridge 405.
Roe Head Trekking Centre, Pooley Bridge. Tel Pooley Bridge 459.

Rookin House Farm, Troutbeck. Tel Greystoke 561.
Side Farm, Patterdale. Tel Glenridding 337.
Troutbeck Hotel, Troutbeck. Tel Greystoke 243.

WESTERN DALES AND COAST

Allonby Riding School, The Hill, Allonby. Tel Allonby 273.
Dock Side Riding School, Station Cottage, Silloth. Tel Silloth 31720.
Fleming Hall, Gosforth. Tel Seascale 455.
Hilltop Farm Riding Centre, Brocklebank, Wigton. Tel Caldbeck 439.
Kynance Farm Trekking Centre, Glasson. Tel Kirkbride 388.
Low Cock How Farm, Kinniside, Cleator. Tel Lamplugh 354.
Marron Trekking Centre, Bridgefoot. Tel Workington 61448.
Midtown Riding Centre, Seaton Road, Broughton Moor. Tel Maryport 3696.
Silloth Riding School, Silloth. Tel Silloth 667.

FURNESS AND CARTMEL

Bigland Hall Riding Centre, Backbarrow. Tel Newby Bridge 728.
Guides Farm, Cart Lane, Grange-over-Sands. Tel Grange 2165.

Mrs. J. Rogers, Birkby Cottage, Cartmel. Tel Cartmel 319.

CARLISLE AND THE EDEN VALLEY

Ash Lea, Murton, Appleby. Tel Appleby 51259.
Cargo Riding School, Cargo. Tel Rockcliffe 300.
Castle Carrock Riding Centre, Weary Sportsman Inn, Castle Carrock. Tel Hayton 230.
Fox Inn Trekking Centre, Ousby. Tel Langwathby 374.
Grey Horse Riding Stables, Brough. Tel Kirkby Stephen 71263.
Rectory Farm, Ormside. Tel Appleby 51110.
Scotby School of Equitation, Scotby Greensteading. Tel Scotby 392.
Stonerigg Riding Centre, Great Orton. Tel Burgh-by-Sands 253.
Stoneriggs, Hilton. Tel Appleby 51354.

SOUTH-EAST CUMBRIA

Greenhills Stables, Crook. Tel Staveley 821327.
Hipshow Farm, Patton. Tel Kendal 23341.
Hollins Farm Riding Centre, Far Arnside, Silverdale. Tel Silverdale 701767.
Holmescales Riding School, Old Hutton. Tel Kendal 22292.
Kendal Riding School, Kendal Parks Farm. Tel Kendal 22087.

Boating and Sailing

There are regular 'steamer' services on Windermere (Lakeside - Bowness - Waterhead); Ullswater (Pooley Bridge - Glenridding); Derwentwater (from Boat Landings, Lake Road, Keswick); and Coniston Water in the restored steam yacht 'Gondola'. The following firms offer boat hire facilities:-

CONISTON WATER

Coniston Boating Centre, Lake Road, Coniston. Motor boats, rowing boats, sailing dinghies.

DERWENTWATER

Keswick-on-Derwentwater Launch Co Ltd, 29 Manor Road, Keswick. Motor boats, rowing boats.
Nichol End Marine, Portinscale. Motor boats, rowing boats.

GRASMERE

J. D. Allonby, Padmire, Pavement End, Grasmere. Rowing boats.

LOWESWATER

Kirkstile Inn, Loweswater. Rowing boats.

ULLSWATER

Tindal (Penrith) Ltd, St Patrick's Boat Landing, Lakeside, Glenridding. Motor boats.
Ullswater Sailing School, Landends, Watermillock. Sailing cruisers.

WINDERMERE

Ambleside Motor Launch Co, Waterhead. Motor boats, rowing boats.
Bowness Bay Boating Co Ltd, Bowness. Motor boats, rowing boats.
Windermere Lake Holidays Afloat Ltd, Bowness. Motor boats, day sailers.
Fell Foot Country Park, Newby Bridge (National Trust). Rowing boats, yachts.
Huddleston & Dixon, Newby Bridge. Rowing boats.

Indoor Lakeland

(including the surrounding areas of Cumbria)

Visitor Centres

BORROWDALE—Lake District National Park Dalehead Base: Converted barn at Seatoller with interesting displays and study facilities. Daily, Easter to October.

GRIZEDALE FOREST Visitor & Wildlife Centre: 3 miles south of Hawkshead. Displays explain many aspects of forestry operations including related subjects such as industrial archaeology and wildlife. See also 'Country Parks and Nature Trails' and 'Museums and Art Centres'. Open daily.

SEDBERGH—Yorkshire Dales National Park Centre: Alongside the Joss Lane car park. Interpretive displays of Sedbergh, Dentdale and Garsdale. Daily, Easter to October.

WHINLATTER Visitor Centre: On Whinlatter Pass on the B5292 Keswick - Lorton - Cockermouth road. Displays and audio-visual presentations of various facets of forestry work. See also 'Country Parks and Nature Trails'. Daily, Easter to October.

WINDERMERE—Lake District National Park Centre: At Brockhole on the A591 Ambleside road two miles north of Windermere. Audiovisual exhibitions on local geology, geography and history. Comprehensive programme of talks and films. Terraced cafeteria. See also 'Country Parks and Nature Trails'. Daily, mid-March to end of October.

Historic Houses

AMBLESIDE—Rydal Mount: Off the A591 between Ambleside and Grasmere. Wordsworth's home from 1813 until his death in 1850, it is still owned by a descendant. The building incorporates a 16th century farmer's cottage; it contains family portraits, furniture and many of the poet's personal possessions. See also 'Gardens'. Daily, beginning of March to end of October, 10.0am - 5.30pm; also November to mid-January, 10.0am - 12.30pm, 2.0pm - 4.0pm.

APPLEBY—Flass House: At Maulds Meaburn, south-west of Appleby off the B6260 Tebay road. Early Victorian house in Palladian style. Permanent Oriental exhibition including Chinese porcelain and opium smoking accessories. Thursdays and Sundays in summer, 2.0pm - 5.0pm.

CARNFORTH—Leighton Hall: Home of the Gillow family for several generations and containing many fine examples of their early furniture. 18th century house with Gothic facade framed against a backcloth of Lakeland hills. Cafe with home-made cakes. See also 'Gardens' and 'Country Parks and Nature Trails'. May to end of September, Wednesdays, Thursdays and Sundays, 2.0pm - 5.0pm.

COCKERMOUTH—Wordsworth House: Birthplace of the poet William Wordsworth. Audiovisual display and static exhibition in the stables. Light refreshments in the old kitchen. National Trust property. Beginning of April to end of October, weekdays (except Thursdays) 11.0am - 5.0pm, Sundays 2.0pm - 5.0pm.

CONISTON—Brantwood: On the east side of Coniston Water, 2½ miles from Coniston village. Home of John Ruskin from 1872 until 1900. Items on display include pictures by Ruskin as well as his coach, boat and much of his furniture. See also 'Country Parks and

Nature Trails'. Daily (except Saturdays), Easter to end of October, 11.0am - 5.30pm.

DALTON Castle: 14th century square tower at head of main street in Dalton-in-Furness. Houses collection of armour and local records. National Trust property. Open daily.

GRASMERE—Dove Cottage: See 'Museums and Art Centres'.

HOLKER Hall: Just off the B5278 Haverthwaite -Cark road. 16th century house with 19th century additions, once the favourite home of the Dukes of Devonshire. Attractions include a countryside museum and aquarium, motor museum, craft and industry exhibition, baby animal farm, collectors' galleries, model railway and adventure playground. There are regular monthly special park events in the season. Gift shop, home-made food in cafeteria. See also 'Gardens'. Daily (except Saturdays), Easter to end of September, 11.0am - 6.0pm.

KENDAL—Castle Dairy: 14th century building with 12th century floor in kitchen. Situated in Wildman Street, it was originally the dairy farm for Kendal Castle. Tuesday afternoons in summer.

KENDAL—Sizergh Castle: 3½ miles south of Kendal near the A6/A591 interchange and two miles from Levens Hall (see below). Home of the Strickland family for 700 years, the building is basically a 14th century pele tower with 15th, 16th and 18th century additions. Contents include a collection of Stuart portraits and relics. National Trust property. April to end of September, Wednesdays and Sundays (also Thursdays in July and August), 2.0pm - 5.45pm.

LEVENS Hall: Close to the junction of the A6 with the A590 Barrow road. Elizabethan house of exceptional interest with fine panelling, plaster work and notable furniture. A collection of steam engines is under steam on open days, and on Sundays a number of traction engines are in steam. Gift shop, light refreshments. See also 'Gardens'. Easter to end of September, Tuesdays, Wednesdays, Thursdays and Sundays, 2.0pm - 5.0pm.

NEWBY BRIDGE—Rusland Hall: 3 miles north-west of Newby Bridge on minor road to Hawkshead. Georgian mansion with permanent exhibition of musical instruments, photographic equipment and other curios. Daily, beginning of April to beginning of October, 11.0am - 6.0pm.

PENRITH—Dalemain: 3 miles south-west of Penrith on A592 Ullswater road. Historic home of the Hasell family with pele tower, banqueting hall and Tudor extensions behind imposing Georgian facade. Countryside museum; Westmorland and Cumberland Yeomanry Museum; display of agricultural bygones. Gift shop, tea room. Daily (except Fridays), Easter to end of September, 2.0pm - 5.15pm.

PENRITH—Hutton-in-the-Forest: 5 miles north-west of Penrith on B5305 Wigton road. 14th century pele tower with later additions of great architectural interest. Pictures, tapestry and furniture over 4½ centuries. Gift shop, tea room. Thursdays, end of May to end of September (also Bank Holiday Mondays), 2.0pm - 5.0pm.

RAVENGLASS—Muncaster Castle: Dates back to 13th century pele tower built on Roman foundations. Superb collection of tapestries, china and pictures including work by Gainsborough, Reynolds and Van Dyck. 16th and 17th century furniture and library of over six thousand books. Children's playground, tea rooms, gift shop. See also 'Gardens'. Easter to beginning of October, Tuesdays, Wednesdays, Thursdays and Sundays, 2.0pm - 5.0pm.

SAWREY: Hill Top: Behind the Tower Bank Arms at Near Sawrey. The house in which Mrs William Heelis (Beatrix Potter) wrote her 'Peter Rabbit' books. National Trust property, preserved almost exactly as she left it. April to end of October, weekdays (except Fridays) 10.0am - 5.30pm, Sundays 2.0pm - 5.30pm. Numbers may be restricted owing to the small size of the house—considerable delays can occur at peak visiting times.

TROUTBECK—Townend: 17th century 'statesman's house' with carved woodwork and many possessions of the yeoman family who lived here until 1944. National Trust property. Daily (except Saturdays and Mondays), April to end of October, 2.0pm - 6.0pm or dusk if earlier.

ULVERSTON—Conishead Priory: Off A5087 road between Ulverston and Bardsea. Large 19th century Gothic house on site of 12th century Augustinian priory now being restored by the Manjushri Institute, a college of buddhist studies. Displays of traditional Tibetan art and culture. Cafe with home-baked refreshments and craft shop. Easter to October, Wednesdays, Thursdays and weekends, 2.0pm - 5.0pm.

ULVERSTON—Swarthmoor Hall: Elizabethan house famed as the birthplace of Quakerism and for its associations with George Fox. Mid-March to October, Mondays, Tuesdays, Wednesdays and Saturdays, 10.0am - noon, 2.0pm - 5.0pm.

WINDERMERE—Belle Isle: Built in 1778 on the 30 acre island in the middle of Windermere. Interior by the Adams brothers, portraits by Romney and furniture by Gillow. Access by boat from Bowness. See also 'Gardens' and 'Country Parks and Nature Trails'. Mid-May to mid-September, Sundays, Mondays, Tuesdays and Thursdays, 10.30am - 5.0pm.

Churches

ABBEY TOWN—Holm Cultram Abbey: Near the junction of the B5307 Carlisle - AbbeyTown and B5392 Wigton - Silloth roads. The present structure is only part of the original abbey church which was larger than Carlisle Cathedral. Fine Norman west doorway with dog-tooth moulding. Timber roof is probably original.

BEETHAM Church: Just off the A6 Kendal to Carnforth road. Battlemented church with Saxon foundations. Double piscina in the Beetham chapel; 15th century glass in the west window of the tower.

BOLTON Church: Off the A66 north-west of Appleby. Norman doorways on north and south sides; nave of late Norman period.

BROUGHAM—Parish Church of Ninekirks: Fascinating small church on south-east side of Penrith, completely rebuilt by Lady Anne Clifford in 1660 in defiance of Oliver Cromwell. 16th and 18th century brasses of members of the Brougham family and 12th century grave covers. Much 17th century wood carving.

CALDBECK Church: Famed for its associations with John Peel whose grave is in the churchyard. Inside the church there is a 13th century leper window on the north side of the chancel. The wall behind the choir seats is Norman.

CARLISLE Cathedral: Dating from about 1130 and especially notable for its fine east window and the 15th century choir stalls with painted backs and exquisitely carved misericords and canopies. The 16th century screen and beautiful painted roof are other outstanding features. The Border Regiment Chapel has massive columns and clerestory with Norman windows and capitals, probably built with stones from Hadrian's Wall.

CARTMEL Priory: The central tower, with the upper stage placed diagonally over the lower, is an architectural curiosity. Inside, this beautiful church of the former priory contains a splendid roof, carved screen and choir stalls with canopies. The misericords survived 80 years of weathering during the post-dissolution period when the church was stripped.

CROSTHWAITE Church: On the north side of Keswick. Has nine unique consecration crosses marking the re-dedication of this Norman church in the 16th century. In the Mary Magdalene Chapel is the fine Radcliffe memorial of 1527 with brasses about two feet long. There is also a memorial to Robert Southey who preceded Wordsworth as Poet Laureate. Other ancient curiosities in the church include the 14th century font, 15th century effigies and an ancient pillow stone.

DACRE Church: West of Penrith to the north of the A592. Norman nave and chancel with 13th century lancet windows and square-headed priest's door.

GOSFORTHChurch: Just off the A595 coast road east of the village. Parts of the building are probably pre-Norman. At the west end of the north aisle are two hogback tombstones of the 10th century. For details of the Gosforth cross see 'Places of Historic Interest'.

GRASMERE Church: In the churchyard are the graves of William Wordsworth, his wife Mary, his sister Dorothy and daughter Dora. Nearby is the grave of Hartley Coleridge. Inside the church, the Wordsworth memorial is in the nave.

GREAT SALKELD Church: On B6412 Penrith to Lazonby road. Magnificent Norman doorway with three recessed orders with carvings including beak-head, zig-zag and emblems of Scandinavian mythology. Tower was built in 1380 as a fortification against Scots raiders.

GREYSTOKE Church: Large and spacious church with 15th century chancel screen, canon stalls and misericords. East window contains stained glass of the same period.

ISEL Church: Alongside river Derwent between Cockermouth and Bassenthwaite. Small Norman church with many interesting features —south doorway with zig-zag mouldings, unique pre-Conquest Triskele Stone with three-armed carving and a spiral staircase which does not lead anywhere!

KENDAL Church: Holy Trinity is the largest parish church in England and has a history dating back to the 9th century. Over 100 feet wide, its four rows of pillars make an impressive sight. In the Bellingham chapel is a brass of 1533.

KIRKBY LONSDALE Church: Still retains its great west Norman doorway, richly carved in four recessed orders. The Norman pillars inside the church are outstanding. In the churchyard is a gazebo giving extensive views over the Lune valley; this panorama was painted by Turner and praised by Ruskin.

KIRKOSWALD Church: On the B6413 Penrith - Brampton road. Notable for its detached tower which stands on top of the hill behind the

church. It was probably thus positioned so that the bells could be heard in several directions.

LONG MARTON Church: North of Appleby. Of Saxon origins with Norman alterations. Two tympana (filled heads of doorways) depict winged animals and twisted birds' heads.

MILLOM Church: Built on the site of a former chapel, the north doorway being reached by a drawbridge across the moat. Parts of the nave and chancel are 12th century. The fish or vesica window in the west wall of the Hudleston chapel is of unique design.

OVER DENTON Church: To the north of the A69 between Brampton and Greenhead. One of the earliest churches in Britain, probably built with stones from the deserted Roman camp of Amboglana across the river Irthing. Chancel has an original Roman arch—one of only two in existence. The nave—little larger than the average living room—has a Saxon doorway and also a blocked-up Devil's Door.

PENRITH Church: Norman tower with walls six feet thick. In the churchyard are stones marking the Giant's grave—supposedly that of Owain, king of Cumbria about 920-37.

ST BEES Church: The fine Norman abbey church of St Bees Priory, built of a deep red sandstone. Zig-zag and beak-head mouldings can be discerned on the west doorway. The capital headings on the arches beneath the tower are rare examples of 12th century work.

SHAP—Keld Chapel: One mile south-west of Shap village close to river Lowther. Small 15th century building with east window of special interest. National Trust property.

WETHERAL Church: On B6263 south-east of Carlisle. 13th century round piers in the chancel and 15th century glass in the west window of the tower. The Howard chapel has many interesting features. The ancient oak tree near the church door is reputed to be a thousand years old.

Museums and Art Centres

BARROW-IN-FURNESS—Furness Museum: In Ramsden Square. Covers all aspects of the Furness area. Includes the Vickers-Armstrong collection of ship models. Weekdays 10.0am - 5.0pm (1.0pm on Thursdays and Saturdays).

BRAMPTON—LYC Museum and Art Gallery: Converted farmhouse at Banks on the Roman wall. Permanent exhibition of Roman and other antiquities, along with the works of international artists. Sculpture garden and an arts

92

room where visitors can participate by attempting to paint their own works! Refreshment facilities. Daily, 9.0am - 7.0pm.

BRAMPTON—Sands House Curio Museum: Collection of fairground amusements (including an organ), stamps, postcards, toys and other curios.

CARLISLE—Border Regiment Museum: In Queen Mary's Tower, Carlisle Castle. Cumbria's military museum depicting the history of the regiment over the last three centuries. Uniforms, medals, weapons, trophies and documents are on display. For opening hours see 'Places of Historic Interest' —Carlisle Castle.

CARLISLE—Guildhall Museum: In The Guildhall, Greenmarket. Displays of guild, civic and local history. Weekdays 10.0am - 6.0pm (4.0pm October to April).

CARLISLE Museum & Art Gallery: Tullie House, Castle Street. Important regional collection of archaeology and natural history; a national centre for the study of Roman Britain and British birds. Good collection of paintings and English porcelain. Weekdays 9.0am - 7.0pm (5.0pm October to March); also Sundays in June, July and August 2.30pm - 5.0pm.

CARNFORTH—Steamtown: See 'Steam Railways'.

CARTMEL—Michael Gibbon Gallery: Barn gallery and workshop featuring the artist's own wood sculptures.

CARTMEL—Old Smithy: Old hearths, tools and equipment have been preserved as they were when last used over a decade ago. Special collection of horse shoes and other mementoes.

CONISTON—Ruskin Museum: Yewdale Road, Coniston. Illustrates the life and work of John Ruskin; also includes items relating to local history and scenery. Easter to end of October, 10.0am - dusk.

ESKDALE—Eskdale Mill, Boot: 16th century restored corn mill with permanent exhibition on the history and technique of milling. Visitors are asked to use the car park at Dalegarth station, ¼ mile west. Daily (except Saturdays), Easter to end of October, 11.0am - 5.0pm.

ESKDALE—Muncaster Mill: Just off A595 coast road north of Ravenglass and alongside Muncaster Halt on Ravenglass & Eskdale Railway. Fully restored working water mill producing stone-ground flour. Open summer months only.

GRASMERE—Dove Cottage: On east side of A591 south of Grasmere village. The early home of Wordsworth from 1799 until 1808, it remains almost as it was in his time and contains some of his furniture and personal possessions. Weekdays, Easter to October, 9.30am - 5.30pm.

GRASMERE—Wordsworth Museum: Town End, Grasmere. Personal relics, manuscripts and a collection of objects illustrating rural life in Wordsworth's time. Opening hours as Dove Cottage.

GRIZEDALE Deer Museum: At Grizedale Forest Visitor & Wildlife Centre—see 'Visitor Centres'. Daily, beginning of May to beginning of October, 11.0am - 5.0pm (opens at 2.0pm on Mondays and Thursdays).

HAWKSHEAD Courthouse: On the north side of Hawkshead on the B5286 Ambleside road. Displays show many aspects of local domestic and folk life, especially swill-making and weaving. Daily (except Mondays), May to mid-October, 2.0pm - 5.0pm.

HOLKER Hall—Lakeland Motor Museum: Large collection of cars, motor cycles, tricycles, bicycles and model cars as well as replica of 1930 garage and collections of automobilia. For opening hours see 'Historic Houses'.

KENDAL—Abbot Hall Art Gallery: 18th century furnished rooms and modern galleries with pictures, sculpture and pottery. Regular programme of exhibitions. Weekdays 10.30am - 5.30pm; Saturdays and Sundays 2.0pm - 5.0pm.

KENDAL—Abbot Hall Museum of Lakeland Life and Industry: Excellent displays of social and economic history including period rooms, costume, farming, local industries, weaving and printing. Craft shop. Weekdays 10.30am - 12.30pm, 2.0pm - 5.0pm; Saturdays and Sundays 2.0pm - 5.0pm.

KENDAL—Brewery Arts Centre: In Highgate. Photographic gallery and exhibitions. Restaurant and bar. Daily (except Sundays) 9.0am - 11.0pm.

KENDAL Museum of Archaeology & Natural History: Station Road. Outstanding collections of mammals and birds; new gallery of Lakeland natural history. Monday to Friday, 10.30am - 5.0pm; Saturdays 2.0pm - 5.0pm.

KESWICK—Fitz Park Museum & Art Gallery: Contains original manuscripts by Wordsworth, Coleridge, Southey and Walpole. Also geological and natural history items of local interest. Weekdays, April to October, 10.0am -

12.0 noon, 2.0pm - 5.0pm (7.0pm in July and August).

LANGWATHBY—Little Salkeld Water Mill: One mile from Langwathby, north of A686 Penrith - Alston road. 18th century corn mill restored to full working order and usually in operation at opening times. Freshly milled wholemeal flour available. Tearoom and shop. Easter to end of October, Wednesdays, Thursdays and Saturdays (also Fridays in August), 2.30pm - 5.30pm.

MARYPORT Maritime Museum: Senhouse Street. Items of maritime interest with particular relevance to the Maryport area. Tuesday to Saturday, 10.0am -12.0 noon, 2.0pm - 4.0pm.

MILLOM Folk Museum: St George's Road. Unique full scale model of a drift of the former Hodbarrow iron ore mine. Also miner's cottage kitchen and blacksmith's forge. End of May to mid-September, weekdays 10.0am - 5.0pm, Sundays 2.0pm - 5.0pm.

MILNTHORPE—Heron Corn Mill: At Beetham, south of Milnthorpe on A6. Car park is at Henry Cook's mills from where there is a footpath. Restored 18th century mill with exhibition about the history of the building and the milling process. Daily (except Mondays), beginning of April to end of September, 11.0am - 12.15pm, 2.0pm - 5.0pm.

ULVERSTON—Laurel and Hardy Museum: Upper Brook Street. Pictures, photographs and books associated with Laurel's home town including furniture from his house. Summer months only, 10.0am - 4.0pm.

WHITEHAVEN MUSEUM: In the Market Place. Special emphasis on mining and maritime history and Whitehaven pottery. Temporary exhibitions. Weekdays 10.0am - 5.0pm.

WINDERMERE Steamboat Museum: Rayrigg Road, Bowness. Houses a unique collection of Victorian and Edwardian steam launches, including the oldest mechanically-powered boat in the world. Changing displays feature other historical craft, the story of life on the lake, its people and pastimes. Lake trips by steam launch subject to weather and availability. Easter to October, weekdays 10.0am - 5.0pm, Sundays 2.0pm - 5.0pm.

WORKINGTON—Carnegie Theatre and Arts Centre: Finkle Street. Arts centre staging exhibitions. Weekdays 10.0am - 5.30pm (10.30 pm on Tuesdays).

WORKINGTON—Helena Thompson Museum: Park End Road. Victorian objects, costumes, furniture, ceramics and other items of local interest. Tuesday to Saturday, 10.0am - 12.0 noon, 2.0pm - 4.0pm.

Steam Railways

LAKESIDE & HAVERTHWAITE RAILWAY: 3½ mile long preserved standard gauge railway running through the beautiful Leven valley. Locomotives and rolling stock are based at Haverthwaite. Trains run in connection with the Windermere steamers at Lakeside. Open summer months only.

RAVENGLASS & ESKDALE RAILWAY: 15-inch gauge line climbing for seven miles from the coast at Ravenglass to Dalegarth, ¼ mile west of Boot. Cafes and shops; railway museum at

Ravenglass. Daily service, beginning of April to beginning of November.

STEAMTOWN: The largest railway centre in the north-west, based on the former engine sheds at Carnforth. Access from Warton Road. Home of 'Flying Scotsman', 'Sir Nigel Gresley' and some thirty other British and Continental locomotives and coaches. Passenger services operate daily in July and August, also Sundays Easter to October. Steamtown is open daily 9.30am - 6.0pm (4.30pm in winter).

A Lakeland Calendar

The following are some of the more important traditional events in Lakeland and Cumbria. Fuller details are available from information centres.

JUNE

APPLEBY Horse Fair: Second Tuesday and Wednesday.

WARCOP Rushbearing: St Peter's Day (June 29th) or preceding Saturday if the 29th is a Sunday.

KESWICK Festival: Date flexible.

JULY

AMBLESIDE Rushbearing: First Saturday.

MUSGRAVE Rushbearing: First Saturday.

HOLKER Hall—Lakeland Rose Show: Second weekend.

CARLISLE—Cumberland Show: Thursday—date flexible.

PENRITH Show: Saturday—date flexible.

AUGUST

AMBLESIDE Sports: Thursday before first Monday.

COCKERMOUTH Show: Saturday before first Monday.

GRASMERE Rushbearing: Saturday nearest St Oswald's Day (August 5th).

CARTMEL Show: Second Wednesday.

GOSFORTH Show: Third Wednesday.

GRASMERE Sports: Third Thursday after first Monday.

PENRITH—Skelton Show: Third Saturday.

CARLISLE Great Fair: From August 26th, usually for one week.

PATTERDALE Sheep Dog Trials: Bank Holiday Saturday.

KESWICK Show: Bank Holiday Monday.

ENNERDALE Show: Last Wednesday.

KENDAL Gathering: Late August/early September.

SEPTEMBER

HAWKSHEAD Show: First Tuesday.

KENDAL—Westmorland Show: Second Thursday.

EGREMONT Crab Fair: Third Saturday.

ULVERSTON—Urswick Rushbearing: Saturday nearest St Michael's Day (September 27th).

ESKDALE Show: Last Saturday.

BROUGH HILL Fair: September 30th.

OCTOBER

WASDALE Show: Second Saturday.

WIGTON Horse Sale: Last Wednesday.

*   *   *

THEATRES AND ENTERTAINMENT CENTRES

BARROW Civic Halls: Duke Street. Tel Barrow 21250.

CARLISLE—Art College Theatre: Carlisle College of Art and Design, Brampton Road. Tel Carlisle 25333.

CARLISLE—City Hall: Castle Street. Tel Carlisle 22232.

CARLISLE—Market Hall: Tel Carlisle 22232.

GRIZEDALE—Theatre in the Forest: Tel Satterthwaite 291.

KENDAL—Brewery Arts Centre: Highgate. Tel Kendal 25133.

KESWICK—Century Theatre: Lakeside Car Park. Tel Keswick 72282.

ULVERSTON—Renaissance Theatre Trust: The Centre, Fountain Street. Tel Ulverston 52299.

WHITEHAVEN—Sir Nicholas Sekers Theatre: At Rosehill, Moresby. Tel Whitehaven 2422.

WORKINGTON—Carnegie Theatre & Arts Centre: Finkle Street. Tel Workington 2122.

For Further Information

There are numerous information centres in Lakeland and Cumbria from where fuller details of items mentioned in this section can be obtained. A selected list is given below:-

AMBLESIDE: Lake District National Park Information Centre, The Old Courthouse, Church Street.

AMBLESIDE: National Trust Information Centre, Bridge House.

APPLEBY: Moot Hall, Boroughgate.

BARROW-IN-FURNESS: Civic Halls, Duke Street.

BOWNESS: Lake District National Park Information Centre, Bowness Bay.

CARLISLE: The Old Town Hall, Green Market.

COCKERMOUTH: Riverside Car Park.

GRANGE-OVER-SANDS: Council Offices, Main Street.

GRASMERE: National Trust Information Centre, Church Stile.

GRIZEDALE: Forestry Commission Information Centre.

HAWKSHEAD: National Trust Information Centre, The Square.

KENDAL: Town Hall, Highgate.

KESWICK: Lake District National Park Information Centre, Moot Hall. Market Square.

KESWICK: National Trust Information Centre, Lakeside.

NEWBY BRIDGE: National Trust Information Centre, Fell Foot Country Park.

PENRITH: Robinson's School, Middlegate.

SEDBERGH: Yorkshire Dales National Park Information Centre, Main Street.

WINDERMERE: Lake District National Park Centre, Brockhole.

OLD FOOTBRIDGE
WATERHOUSES, NR SOULBY
Probably 16th Century